The Beauty

Mrs. Wilson Woodrow

[ZHINGOORA CLASSICS]

[ZHINGOORA BOOKS]

This book edition is published by
Zhingoora Books.

The Cover is Designed by Pallav Sethiya.

CONTENTS

CHAPTER I

A BACHELOR'S BRIDE

If the proper statistics of bachelorhood were accurately tabulated they would show that at certain fixed and recurring periods, a confirmed old bachelor, say one in every ten, casts his dearly-bought experience, his hard-won knowledge of the world and women to the four winds of heaven, and chooses for himself a wife; and, as his friends and relatives invariably protest, a bungling job he makes of it. He may, before the world, walk soberly, discreetly, advisedly and in the fear of God in every other respect, but when it comes to selecting a companion for the rest of his life, he follows, apparently, a predestined leading, some errant and tricksy impulse, and from a world of desirable and waiting helpmates, eminently suitable, he will, in nine cases out of ten, fix his heart upon the one inevitable She who can keep the pot of trouble ever boiling for him.

This, according to Mr. Cresswell Hepworth's old and intimate friends, was exactly the course which he had followed; nor was even one voice upraised in dissent from this opinion, as they frankly discussed the matter over their champagne and truffled sweetbreads at the breakfast following the wedding.

It was but natural that they who were rarely in complete agreement on any subject which commended itself for discussion among them, should hold a unanimous opinion on this matter which involved the happiness of their lifelong friend. But although the opinion was unanimous, it was not unprejudiced. Hepworth had had his distinct niche in their

4

homes and hearts for many years, and now as they gazed metaphorically at the empty space, it struck a chill to their affections.

Nevertheless they did not, could not fail to join in the little gasp of admiration which breathed through the church as the bride swept up the aisle on the arm of Mr. Willoughby Hewston, the well-known banker and intimate friend of the bride-groom. She had been stopping, it was understood, with Mrs. Wilstead, another friend of Hepworth's, for several weeks.

There were those in the large audience who saw a certain pathos in the fact that she was given away by one of Hepworth's friends, thus exposing the lack of either relatives or friends of her own, but there was nothing in her bearing to indicate that she was conscious of her isolated position as she advanced, leaning lightly on Mr. Hewston's arm.

The world, Hepworth's world, and it was a large one, was tingling with curiosity. He was a great figure, looming immense upon the financial horizon; but no one had ever heard of the bride. The invitations to the wedding were the first intimation of his impending marriage, and the bride's name, Perdita Carey, conveyed nothing to anybody. By dint of careful collection of scraps of information, it gradually became known that she was young, of southern birth and extremely pretty. Bare facts. No more.

It was also considered rather an odd reading of the customary conventions on Hepworth's part, this crowded church wedding exposing the bride's poverty in relatives, the breakfast to follow, at his town house, thus making equally plain her homeless state; but when this view was set before him, sighingly, by Isabel Hewston, and vivaciously by Alice Wilstead, he became obstinate in the insistence of his plans.

5

He seemed possessed of some masculine idea of getting things over, of having all his friends meet his wife en masse, so to speak, and having the matter settled.

And so it was, "Nice customs curtsy to great kings"—or millionaires. The audience then of his friends—there was none of hers present, if indeed she possessed any—sat with heads turned at an aching angle and awaited, with concealed impatience, the choice of Cresswell Hepworth.

The weight of opinion leaned to a sunburst of a woman, darkly splendid, opulently graceful, and instead, when the stately strains of the wedding-march echoed through the church, the guests lifted their astonished eyes to a brown and slender girl; but no matter what the expectation had been, each realized that he gazed on a more poetic loveliness than he had dreamed.

Another unhesitating mental admission. Obscure, unknown she might have been, but she could never be considered ordinary. It had taken generations of cultivation to give that pose of the head and shoulders, that arch of the instep, that taper to her slender wrist. And what intimation of individuality! Few women could have borne more regally the weight of heavy and lusterless satin or a diadem of flashing jewels; but this girlish bride of a millionaire had insisted on being married in the white muslin her own scanty purse had furnished; and wore as if it were a crown of diamonds the wreath of white jasmine flowers which held her long tulle veil close about the cloudy masses of her hair.

For once the entire interest of any occasion which he happened to grace was not centered on Hepworth, who, with his usual invincible composure, awaited the bride at the altar, fortified by his best man, Wallace Martin.

But the owner of millions—unctuous sound—is worth more than a mere dismissing word. Let the bride continue to advance, he to await her, while he is presented in a lightning sketch.

Cresswell Hepworth was far from old, not fifty. He had more than three generations of cultivated ancestry behind him. In type he was American, approaching the Indian; tall, slightly aquiline of feature, somewhat granitic and imperturbable. His hair, which had been brown, was almost white, his eyes were gray, trained to express nothing, but startlingly penetrating when he chose to lift rather heavy lids with a peculiarly long droop at the corners.

Emerson says somewhere that "a feeble man can see the farms that are fenced and tilled, the houses that are built. The strong man sees the possible houses and farms. His eye makes estates as fast as the sun breeds clouds."

Hepworth was a strong man. He saw possible houses and farms, externalized them and became the acquirer of vast and profitable tracts of land—a fair map blackly dotted with mines and scrawled with the angular lines of intersecting railroads. In this yellow triangle, a great wheat farm. Here, in this square of living green, irrigated and profitable ranches. He stood, this "Colossus of Finance"—journalese—with his feet planted firmly on this solid map-basis, and, with a golden rake, drew toward him from countless clutching hands securities, stocks, bonds, curios, pictures (he was an ardent collector), loot of every description, and, it was even whispered through the church, his young and lovely bride.

But now he stepped forward to meet her with a smile that enlivened his whole face, even his eyes. The service flowed on. With that air of sulky geniality which represented his most urbane manner, Willoughby Hewston gave away the bride.

7

The responses were duly made, and Mr. and Mrs. Cresswell Hepworth turned to walk through an aisle of smiling and nodding friends.

At that moment the mellow October sunlight fell through the stained windows enwrapping Perdita in a regal and impalpable vesture of scarlet and gold; and again a murmur of admiration rippled and echoed at this fresh revelation of her beauty. She had been pale as she walked up the aisle, but now her color had risen and the crimson on her brown cheek was the hue of a jacqueminot rose. Her hair, a deep chestnut at the temples, flowed into copper, dark in the hollows, gold where it caught the light. Her coloring was a harmony of all soft, warm, dusky shades, and one looked to the eyes to focus these tints in light or darkly rich topaz; but Perdita's eyes were gray, handed down perhaps from those Irish kings to whom her father had laughingly traced his descent.

"Lucky girl!" murmured Alice Wilstead an hour later to the group of Hepworth's intimate friends who sat together at one table during the breakfast that followed the wedding. "Just think of it. He has no family encumbrances. Never an 'in-law' will she have to cope with."

It never struck her that Hepworth's little circle of close friends had gradually assumed about all of the intrusive and proprietary prerogatives of the nearest and most affectionate relatives.

Alice Wilstead was a widow, dark, slender, piquant, versed in the secrets of grace and the art of wearing her jewels so that they accentuated her sparkling eyes and her one precious dimple without eclipsing them. Warmly sympathetic and impulsive, she had been overcome by the vision of Perdita's isolation as the girl walked up the aisle on the grudging arm of Willoughby Hewston; and had pressed her handkerchief lightly to her eyes, a moment of emotion viewed with callous interest by a misinterpreting world which regarded it as a last tear shed for a lost opportunity, a shattered hope.

"Well," said Hewston, finishing his sweetbreads and preparing to begin on the next course, "it went off very well. I was all right, wasn't I?"

"You were perfect, dear," his wife hastened to assure him, "and it was a beautiful wedding."

Mrs. Hewston was gray and pink and plump like her husband; and this morning her grayness and pinkness and plumpness were underlined, thrown into high relief by a violet gauze gown, heavily spangled in silver. Isabel Hewston resembled nothing so much as a comfortable, placid, fireside cat, purry and complacent. If she possessed claws, which is doubtful, they were always well concealed.

"Yes, a beautiful wedding and a beautiful bride," she murmured, with a little sighing inflection habitual to her, "so young, so—"

"Humph!" interrupted her husband, with as much of a snort as a mouthful of game would permit, "I tell you it's a pretty tough thing for all of us to see old Hepworth looking so happy." He thrust out his lower lip and wrinkled up his eyes until he bore a grotesque likeness to a baby about to cry. "Hepworth's my best friend, and to see that look of almost boyish joy on his face was pretty hard. There are some things you can do and some you can't; now one of these things that no man can afford to do is to marry outside his own class. I could have told Cress so."

The other members of this intimate little coterie of friends, five in all, looked at one another and burst into involuntary laughter.

9

Wallace Martin, an old young man, a magazine writer, who would fain be a playwright, gave the single bark of mirth which served him for an explosion of laughter. It sounded particularly derisive now.

"I would give my little all to have the new Mrs. Hepworth hear you say that," he chuckled. "Dear old Hewston, she would not in a thousand years consider any of us in her class. She belonged, let me inform you, to one of the oldest of southern families. Her mother was a cotton princess of the loveliest and haughtiest variety. One of the famous belles of her day. Her father, too, was of the old South."

"Why, what are you talking about?" growled Hewston irascibly. "She hadn't a dime—was a beautiful cloak model or something of that kind."

"She painted dinky things for a living, if you mean that," said Martin carelessly, "lamp-shades and menu cards and such."

"If she only had some friends, even one relative," deplored Mrs. Hewston, "it would look so much—er—nicer, you know. Relatives do add a background." She shook her head regretfully.

"We'll have to be her relatives," said Maud Carmine, a niece of Mrs. Hewston and a plain rather faded young woman of pale and indefinite tints and many angles. Her claim to distinction rested on the fact that she was a drawing-room musician of—strange anomaly—real musical feeling. It was her misfortune always to be explained by those who found her tact, good nature and practical common sense useful, and who drew heavily on them, as, "not attractive looking, you know; but pure gold, and one of the most dependable persons," and this damning tribute of friendship served as an admirable check to further curiosity concerning her. "Yes, we must be her

10

background." Her glance lingered for a moment on Wallace Martin, but he returned it briefly and indifferently.

"A young woman who has just married millions needs no family group," remarked Alice Wilstead lightly. "The most effective background is her husband."

"Gad!" Mr. Hewston put down his knife and fork to glare at her. "The idea of looking at Hepworth as a background. He who has always been in the front of everything. A background! And for a snub-nosed chit of a girl!"

"Oh, Willoughby, dear, not snub-nosed," expostulated his wife mildly.

"Snub-nosed, I said," insisted Willoughby. "Didn't I walk up the aisle with her?"

"Hush, dear, hush," murmured his wife. "Here she comes now."

The bride was leaving. Passing through the handsome, stiff apartments like a white cloud, to make ready for the journey before her, she stopped a moment for a word or two with Maud Carmine as she paused at that table.

Hewston rose reluctantly to his feet. "I once heard of a wedding," he said confidentially and hopefully to Wallace Martin, "where the bride went up to change her gown, and never showed up again."

"Where did she go?" asked Wallace with interest.

"Dunno," returned Willoughby. "Old lover. Fourth dimension. Unexplainable, but fact, I assure you."

CHAPTER II

A FAR WORLD OF DREAMING

The bride had passed through the admiring groups with a smile here, a word there and was already half up the stairway, above the voices, the heavy flower scents, the sentimental melodies which stole from the musicians' bower. On, a white, mystic figure, her veil floating behind her; on, without undue haste, but most eagerly, as if she climbed some mount which led from the world to a desired solitude.

On the first landing she paused, leaning for a moment, Juliet-like as from a balcony, and looked down on the moving mosaic of color beneath, the gay, light tones of the women's gowns thrown into relief by the dark coats of the men. The gazers paid her the tribute of involuntary "Ohs," and barely restrained themselves from applause as if at the appearance of their favorite actress. As usual Perdita had made a picture of herself, an involuntary and unpremeditated picture; but in effect beyond the calculations of the most vigilant stage manager.

She stood with one arm lightly upraised holding her bouquet of white jasmine above her laughing face. Behind her, a stained glass window, before her the marble balustrade. Then the bouquet, its white ribbons waving and circling, whirled through the air, over the sea of upturned faces and white clutching hands and straight into Alice Wilstead's arms.

With the laughter and clamor of voices ringing in her ears, Perdita, hidden from sight now by a turn of the staircase, followed, with unconcealed haste, the crimson velvet pathway which led to solitude.

At the top of the stairs she hesitated briefly, glancing right and left. She had been in the house but twice before, both times under the chaperonage of Mrs. Hewston, and she was not sure of the exact geographical position of her own suite of apartments.

At this moment her maid, engaged from that morning, stepped forward and threw open a door. Perdita smiled approval. It would have been difficult to withhold it. Olga, a paragon of maids, if references and experience count, showed no signs of the wear and tear of previous mistresses. She was delightful in appearance, rosy-cheeked, amiable, immaculate, with that air of trained capability which invites confidence.

Perdita paused before entering. "Are all my traveling things out?" she asked.

"Yes, madame."

"Very well, I shall not need you for a few moments. Remain here and when I want you I will ring."

"Yes, madame."

Perdita drew a breath of relief as the door was closed gently behind her. At last she was alone, away from eyes, eyes that were everywhere. She had felt all morning as if she were encompassed by them, appraising eyes, envious eyes, unfamiliar, inquisitive eyes.

She looked slowly about her. And these were her own apartments, these beautiful, cold, unlived-in rooms, as empty of life or individuality as a shell.

Yesterday she had walked through them with Isabel Hewston, pleased, admiring, but a little overawed. She had not realized before what a wizard's wand Cresswell wielded. He had but waved it and great architects and decorators, their disciplined and cultivated imaginations stimulated by the prospect of unlimited expenditure had devised for her, penniless Perdita Carey, all this beauty and luxury. She had only stipulated timidly that she might be environed in her favorite rose color, a mere suggestion for those who had the matter in charge. It was enough. Her bed chamber bloomed with the pale but vivid flush of pink roses, La France, accentuated with cool, suave, silver notes, like the delicate, contrasted phrasing of a musical theme. The result of color and arrangement was youthful, joyous, spacious. Beyond a softly falling curtain, she caught a glimpse of her sitting-room. American beauty, a radiant spot with delicious water colors on the walls, bowls of roses, the sunshine falling through the windows, and shelves of books, each volume bound in creamy vellum.

In one of the long mirrors which reflected her graceful figure from every angle she saw through an opposite door her dressing-room and bath, with its elaborate appointments, more inviting and luxurious than any of which the proudest Roman beauty could have dreamed. She looked about her with a faint, strange smile. What a contrast were these cold and splendid rooms, not yet animated by her personality, to that little apartment with its two or three tiny chambers, high up under the roof, where she had lived and worked!

Then she turned back to her reflection in the mirror. It was extremely becoming to her, all this background of rose and silver. Perdita realized that as she unfastened the white flowers from her hair and let her long veil fall like a cloud about her. With a deft movement she caught it and tossed it on a chair for Olga to fold later. She slipped out of her wedding-gown next and laid it more carelessly still upon a couch. Then she leaned forward, her elbow on the dressing-table, her chin on her hand,

15

and regarded herself steadily, that faint, strange smile still on her lips.

Well, she had fulfilled her destiny, justified Eugene Gresham's prophecy. She heard his words to her, spoken the last time she had seen him, three months before, as plainly as if his voice still rang in her ears.

"Perdita, your destiny is written on your face. It includes marrying a millionaire and having your portrait painted by me."

Fateful words! She had just married the millionaire, but even here, upon the threshold of this new life, she was constrained to halt a moment and cast one backward glance, "just for the old love's sake."

It was the night before Eugene Gresham sailed for Europe to paint the portraits of "Princessin, Contessin and high Altessin." Again she awaited him. Again she heard his step on the stair without, a quick, light step with an odd halt in it.

He was coming, and her heart beat. How it beat as she stood there breathless beside the window!

"Perdita!" Eugene's voice. He was across the room in a flash, both her hands in his. "Here, let me see you in the light." He drew her toward a lamp. "Two years, two years since we have met, and me wasting time painting in the desert places when I might have been with you. Time is not in the Far East. Ah, my cousin!" (the relationship was remote) he sighed. "Why, as I live," with a quick change of tone, "you've got another dimple, and that makes you a new and lovelier Perdita."

She flushed adorably. "How nice and southern," she cried with an attempt at lightness, "and how exactly like you, just like the old 'Gene."

"The old 'Gene," his eyes still holding hers, "has never changed."

"How—how—are the pictures going?" withdrawing her hands from his.

"Beautifully!" he said carelessly. "The glassy eyes of the millionaires are all turning toward me, and I have more commissions to make beautiful on canvas their pug-nosed, fat-faced wives than I care to accept. Those ladies hail me as a great psychological artist. Their mirrors are so cruel to them that when my brushes flatter them they say that I paint their souls; strip away the husk of the flesh and reveal enduring loveliness."

He struck a match to light a cigarette and then hastily shielded it with his cupped hand from the breeze which blew through the open window. The light flared into his down-bent face, bringing out its dissonances almost grotesquely in that small, momentary flash. Pick Gresham to pieces and he was incontrovertibly convicted of sheer ugliness, but the fact bothered him not at all. He knew that few ever arrived at the cool, dispassionate frame of mind regarding him where they were capable of that exhaustive analysis known as picking to pieces. He was slender and rather small of stature, not more than medium height. One shoulder was noticeably higher than the other and he walked with a slight limp, the result of an injury received in boyhood. Coarse, blue-black hair with a sort of crinkle in it stood out from his head like a cloud. His skin was swarthy, his features irregular, even his eyes, dark eyes, were only occasionally brilliant. But he might have been appreciably uglier, almost as hideous as the Yellow Dwarf or

Beauty's Beast,—it would have mattered no more than his present lack of beauty, and well he knew it. His was the magic gift of glamour, and all the dissonances and inharmonies of appearance as well as of character seemed but the italics emphasizing his charm. His mind was supple and flexible, his wits nimble, even subtle. He was as vivid, as veering, as fascinating as flame.

His match, the third he had struck, blew out before it had lighted his cigarette, and he threw it away with a petulant gesture. He did not answer her, as he was again attempting to light his cigarette, this time with success. Then he began to saunter about the room.

In spite of her penury Perdita had yet managed to invest her little workshop with both daintiness and charm. The walls were hung with pink and white chintz and here and there were bits of fragile china and rare old silver on claw-legged mahogany tables, while from dim canvases in tarnished silver frames smiled the sweet, dark eyes of haughty southern beauties of a generation unused to life's struggles.

"You really saved some of the best things from that hideous auction, didn't you?" picking up a bit of china to scrutinize it more carefully. "I was horrified when I heard of it across the world, several months after it was all over. If I'd only been there to buy the whole lot in. Plucky little girl you were, Perdita, to come on here and manage to keep the gaunt, gray wolf at bay."

"What else was there for me to do?" she asked without turning her head. "Aunt died, the place had to go. As for the wolf, if you look sharp, Eugene, you may see his paws thrusting under this door."

18

In the center of the room was a large table covered with paint brushes, colors, a litter of candle shades, cotillion favors and cards in various stages of completion. Eugene carefully cleared a space on that edge of the table nearest Perdita's chair, and perched upon it, looking down at her with a smile.

"My stars, Dita!" he cried with the truest conviction, "you are a beauty! The moment I return, I mean to paint you again. And this time I'll set the world afire. Do you remember how many portraits I have made of you? Why, just to see you brings back my boyhood,—the hopes, the struggles, the effort, the haunted days, the feverish nights. I used to think, 'If I can just learn how to get this effect, I'll know the whole secret.' I've got past that now. There's always a new and more difficult riddle every day. But Dita, Dita, the dreams of my youth you recall!"

The smile died from her face. Her eyes grew wistful. "The dreams of our youth," she repeated. "I'm young yet; but they haunt me. They were beautiful dreams down there on that gray, old river. Can't you shut your eyes, Eugene, and see the terraces sloping down to the water, the lovely, neglected garden with its tangle of roses and jasmine?"

"Do I remember?" His eyes looked deep into hers. "I swear I never smell jasmine without thinking of the old place and you. Perdita, do you ever think what life might have been for us if it hadn't been for our accursed poverty? If we'd only had just a little between us. It's a question of courage. If we'd only had the courage to face things hand in hand we'd have got along somehow, I dare say. But we didn't have that quality, did we? We didn't believe enough in our dreams. That's the worst of life. She won't let you."

"Oh, the dreams!" she scoffed. Her color remained high, her eyes glittered, but with irritation, not tears. She suffered from an old laceration of the heart, the more wounding in that, for

19

pride's sake, she must ever deny it expression. Eugene always took the attitude as if they together had renounced a mutual love, and often implied, without rancor, but with a forgiving, almost understanding tenderness, that the responsibility of their marred lives lay on her shoulders.

Perdita was of the twentieth century, but she was also a southern woman of many traditions, and she could not say the words which rose to her defensive lips: "Eugene, you have never asked me to face life hand in hand with you." He would with a glance, she could see it, feel it, convict her of blunted intuitions, of an inability to discern exquisite shades of emotion; and then he would express his love for her in glowing, passionate phrases, confusingly evasive, elusive beyond definition, committing himself to nothing.

And if this shifting of responsibility on her, this ardent skirting of a definite issue were premeditated or his unavoidable, temperamental way of viewing the matter, she could not tell. Conjecture was idle. Her knowledge of his character, her ready mental accusations and equally ready excuses, these comprising the sole weight of evidence, merely held the scales steady.

Eugene began to pick up, first one, then another, of the favors on the table, a smile, tender yet humorous, about his lips.

"By Jove, these are not so bad! They are rather stunning. You always did have a lot of feeling for form and color, Dita, but you wouldn't work. You weren't willing to drudge and to starve if necessary. That was because you lacked the clear vision. It wasn't always before you, a pillar of cloud by day and a pillar of fire by night." None might doubt his sincerity or conviction now. It was mounting as flame. "Artistic and appreciative you are, Dita. All this trash shows it, but you lack the creative impulse. You were never meant to be a barefooted, tattered follower of the vision, a lodger in a new palace of dreams each night. You should build your house on the rock of substantial things, bread-and-butter facts.

"Oh, do not toss up your head in that wounded-stag manner. Good Lord! Isn't it enough that you are beautiful? And how beautiful! I'm almost tempted to cancel my passage and, instead of sailing to-morrow morning, stop here and paint you again. Really, I am. But what would it profit me? I'd just be sowing the seed for a new harvest of heartaches. Perdita, your destiny is written on your face." It was as if he willed to speak lightly. "It includes marrying a millionaire, and having your portrait painted by me. You'll never have an international reputation as a beauty until you do both." But in spite of his smile and his flippant words there was bitterness in his eyes.

She did not see that, but the lightness of his words and tone pricked her to an immediate decision, a decision which she had, unconsciously, postponed until she had seen him. Her face paled, her lips folded in a tight line.

"I am going to marry the millionaire," she said firmly enough, although there was a slight tremor in her voice. "It depends on you whether or not there is a portrait of Mrs. Cresswell Hepworth by Gresham." There was triumph in her eyes and voice as thus she lifted her pride from the dust.

"Cresswell Hepworth!" His astonishment was unbounded. "Perdita! I throw my hat at your feet. Cresswell Hepworth! The pick of the bunch. Wonderful! But," looking at her curiously, "how on earth did you meet him?"

"He heard of my amulet through a man I met at old Mrs. Huff's, Mr. Martin. He has a wonderful collection of amulets, and he wanted to buy it of me."

"But you didn't sell it?" he said quickly. "No, of course not. H'm-m. That old amulet. You laugh at my superstitions, Dita, but you must admit that it's queer the way it's interwoven with the history of our family."

He began to roll cigarettes and lay them with neat and exquisite regularity on the table beside him. His eyebrows were raised, his mouth twisted in a sort of rueful yet whimsical grimace. When he had finished rolling the sixth cigarette, he laid it in line with the others, an exact line, his eye was so true. Then at last he looked at her, and his cynical, earnest, mocking, enthusiastic face softened. His eyes enveloped her with tenderness. There was a heart-break in his smile.

"Ah, star-eyed Perdita, how shall I give you up? The only woman!" He mused a moment, and then repeated: "The only woman! If we had but had the courage to take the bitter with the sweet, Perdita."

Unwitting goad! It struck too deep for her to conceal the wound.

"You do not say 'can,' I observe, Eugene," she said laughingly, but there was an edge to her voice like that on finely tempered steel.

"No," he returned, his fingers busy with a rearrangement of the cigarettes; "you see it involves you and me. Not John Jones and Jane Smith, but you and me. Do you know what that means? Well, it means that it involves the inheritance and training of a good many generations. Do you think I do not know how you loathe all this?" He flicked with his fingers the dainty trifles on the table. "I know well the craving of your nature for splendor and beauty, how necessary they are to you, and how dinkiness and makeshifts irritate and depress you, take the heart out of you. That is one you, one Perdita. There is another. I saw her when I came in to-night. God, I wish I hadn't!" His voice dropped on this exclamation and she did not hear it. "She is young. Her beautiful, dark eyes ask love and give it. Her heart dreams of it. It is in every tone of her voice. These two are at war, the natural woman and the woman with her inherited love of ease and luxury and cultivated, artificial desires. Which is the stronger? Why, to-night"—he picked up one of the cigarettes and prepared to light it; his hands trembled, his face was white—"the woman who is ready to love. She would listen to me—to-night. I would hold her. Oh, what's the use?" He twisted his shoulders impatiently. Then he bent forward and tapped the table lightly but emphatically, as if to add weight to his words. "You'd listen to me to-night, I know that; but as sure as to-morrow's dawn I'd get a little note from you saying that the morn had brought wisdom. But, oh, I am glad I'm sailing to-morrow."

"So am I," she flashed out. "You think—you take too much for granted, Eugene."

"I dare say." His voice sounded flat. "No one ever appreciates renunciation. Well, it's out into the night in more senses than one." He rose and looked at her as she sat with downcast eyes, and half stretched out his arms toward her. Then as she too rose, he clasped his fingers about the back of her head and drew her face toward him, although she strove to avert it from him. "Good-by, sweetheart." Even she must believe in the ardor and sincerity of his tones. "Good-by, Perdita of the South." He kissed her lightly on one cheek and then the other. "Good-by, my jasmine flower."

He hesitated a moment in leaving the room, as if to turn and clasp her to him and bear her away; then he shut the door gently behind him and she heard his halting, hurried step upon the stair. She sat listening until its last echoes had died away, and then, casting her outstretched arms on the table, sending the favors and menus and candle-shades in a shower to the floor, she burst into a storm of tears.

There was a low, discreet, respectful knock, Olga's knock on the door leading into Mrs. Cresswell Hepworth's splendid apartments. Perdita started violently and came back to the present from her far world of dreaming. She had not even begun to dress, but still was sitting, chin on hand, gazing with apparent intentness at her image in the mirror.

"It is almost time for Madame to start," Olga smiled from the doorway, "so I ventured to remind."

"Yes," Perdita spoke hurriedly, rising at the same time. "Get me into my gown quickly, please, and tie my shoes."

Olga was deft and practised, and Perdita's dressing was the work of a few minutes.

"My veil now," said the new Mrs. Hepworth, "and—oh, I almost forgot." She turned to lift from her dressing-table an exceedingly quaint and striking ornament, depending from a long, thin chain. It was a square of crystal about an inch and a half in diameter, set curiously in strands of silver and gold, twisted and beaten together, and, as must be apparent to even the casual observer, was of ancient and unique workmanship. This was Perdita's amulet, the old charm, which Eugene with his superstitious fancies had always longed to possess, and which had excited also the desire of the collector in Hepworth; but in spite of many temptations to part with it, Dita had always retained possession of it. It was her one link with the past, a personal link, but also a traditional and hereditary one. She wound the chain several times about her neck, and the crystal pendant gleamed dully against the dark blue cloth of her gown.

"You also are ready, Olga?" she said as she passed through the door.

"Yes, Madame."

Hepworth was waiting for Perdita at the head of the stairs. He was in his heavy motoring coat, his cap in hand.

He smiled as he saw her. "Just in time," he said. "I'm afraid we will have to make haste, rather. Ah," as his eye caught the talisman, "you are wearing the amulet, are you not? Blessed old thing. If it had not been for that, I should never have met you."

"I believe you only married me to get it," she replied with an answering smile, "you are such an insatiable collector."

"Do you believe that? Do you?" he asked. "Because if you do, you are as stupid as you are pretty, and you have no idea what that implies."

25

CHAPTER III

PINK AND WHITE EXISTENCE

So Mr. and Mrs. Cresswell Hepworth whirled away in the big motor and for the next few months wandered about the globe. Perdita, who had seen nothing but an old southern plantation and New York, the latter from the curb, as it were, must see everything; so in pursuit of this aim, the Hepworths were constantly stepping from huge, magnificent boats to huge, magnificent motors, thence to huge, magnificent hotels. And cities, the open country, villages, mountain peaks, strange peoples, were as debris strewing the pathway of Perdita's avid flight through new experiences. It was tremendously stimulating, even heady, she found, to hold the world between one's thumb and finger, and turn it this way and that to catch the light. Headier still to discover that to wish is to realize, but proportionately a shock to find that the life of infinite variety may only be lived within circumscribed boundaries. What is more disillusionizing than to learn that money has its limitations? It can merely buy the very best of things, the superlatives of the commonplace, but these, in the last analysis, remain food, lodgings, clothes, conveyances, ornaments, no more. Money can not buy stars or dreams, or love or happiness.

Perdita's soaring youth resented it. But she was adaptable, enormously interested and the ground within the boundaries was new, affording daily opportunities for fresh exploration. And she, quick to observe and compare, had profited by her new experiences. Money became to her merely the medium of exchange for any beautiful thing she might want. Speedily she lost her first, fresh pleasure in making it flutter its little golden wings and fly; but her love of art deepened and strengthened, and at many famous shrines she offered her heart's homage. She took up the study of designing, and worked at it

26

systematically with an ardor and intensity which at first amused and then puzzled her husband.

On their return from their travels Perdita occupied herself in altering, refurnishing and redecorating one or two of Hepworth's country places and his town house. She worked in consultation with a great firm, and succeeded in changing the weary acquiescence of "our Mr. So and So" to interest and an astonishment bordering on enthusiasm. She was not the average rich woman who had gone in for being artistic, with a head full of glaringly impossible ideas and a flow of helpful suggestions which set the professional teeth on edge.

On the contrary, this girl, Mrs. Hepworth, really knew a few things and was willing to learn more. She was a student. "The only woman," murmured dazedly "our Mr. Smith-Jones," "the only woman I ever met who realizes that decoration must conform to architecture, not defy it. You usually have to fracture their skulls to make them understand that pompadour prettinesses are not suitable in a Gothic chapel."

But when she had finished the houses, and designed more costumes than she could wear, she looked about her for fresh worlds to conquer, and discovered that she was up against the boundaries. Walls everywhere! She could do anything she chose, travel, buy clothes, motors, an aëroplane if she wanted it, only she did not. She next went through a phase when she decided that the people with whom she was thrown were intolerable, representing a frivolous and empty-headed society. Her imagination dwelt on the class who "did things," "the dreamers," she called them to herself, who adorned a brilliant, picturesque, delightfully haphazard Bohemia, where, at feasts, principally of red wine and bloomy, purple grapes, laughter pealed to the rafters, and the conversation sparkled as if sprinkled with stardust. She strove to enter this Olympian vagabondia, and found herself entangled in the nets of many

27

fowlers, sycophantic, impecunious, and, unsated of their many banquets, physically hungry.

She began to have seasons of ennui and depression, increasing in frequency. What was the matter with her world? Nothing, she would hasten to assure herself, it was the best of all possible worlds, and she, a darling of fortune—once, unforgetably, the waif of chance—was the most contented of women. Only—what was the matter with this perversely empty and uninteresting world?

It was not always so. It was once invested with wonderful things, and such simple things, too. She remembered how she used to stand at the window of her little work-room watching the day fade, marveling at the miracle of the twilight. While the sun was high, she had seen only commonplace, dusty streets, crowded with people, and had heard only a crazy, creaking old piano-organ grinding away on the pavement beneath, but in the soft indefiniteness of twilight these solid houses and buildings would become unsubstantial, mere shadowy arabesques on the spangled gloom of night. There were purple vistas, glittering lights and fairy towers. She would hold her breath, almost expecting to hear a nightingale. It was all mystery and magic, life and romance, that eternal romance her starved youth asked. How she used to dream of the unexpected, the dazzling unexpected!

And then Cresswell had come, and, as she thought, offered it to her. To do Perdita justice, she had not married Hepworth merely because of his great wealth. She was incapable of such sordid and callous calculation. But Cophetua had met this beggar maid at her most disheartened and despairing moment, and without difficulty had succeeded in first winning her interest and then enchaining her imagination.

28

In her two years of struggle to earn her livelihood Eugene had become more or less a memory, and, in spite of the fascination and interest he had always had for her, she did not blind herself to certain erratic tendencies of his. He might appear at any moment, so she judged him, with vows of eternal love, and straightway, if the mood seized him, begin a new picture and forget her. And so she married Hepworth largely that life might become a successive series of introductions to an ever varying unexpected. Instead, although her quest was feverish, she encountered only the commonplace. She was like a mouse which has discovered the inadequacy of cheese to quench its soul-yearnings. What remained?

The truth of the matter was that Perdita's world, which seemed so hopelessly askew to her, had an architectural defect. It lacked that sure antidote to ennui—a Bluebeard's closet.

Now Perdita was young and healthy. She had great curiosity, and a certain insatiable mental quality which would have successfully riveted her interest to life, but for one fact, her heart was as ardent and insatiable as her intelligence—and her husband bored her. There is no record of Bluebeard boring any of his wives.

She became more and more conscious of a continual little plaint running always through her consciousness, like the sad, monotonous murmur of an ever-flowing stream, a little unceasing plaint against life in the abstract and life in its personal application.

"There must be as many worlds as there are points of view," so ran the stream, "but my life's like a wedding-cake, all white and sparkling and overdecorated, and absolutely insipid. Candy! That's what it is ... my rooms are all pink and white, and I'm crusted over with pink sugar." Perdita always thought in color. "I'm tired of all this pink and white and baby-blue existence. I'd welcome a little scarlet and black sin for a change. Oh, it's just your corsets over again. You're put in them when you're about fifteen and you never get out of them again. We women think in corsets, breathe in them. We live in them mentally, and accept all their constrictions and restrictions as a matter of course. We take in drafts of air, and expand our lungs and say we're emancipated, but we only expand as much as the corsets allow. We've put our world in corsets, to confine us still more ... mine used to be mended, frequently washed, with some of the bones broken; now I have many pairs, brocade, satin—cloth of gold, if I want them—but they are the same thing, corsets, corsets on our bodies and brains and lives.

"Look at Cresswell. He doesn't wear corsets. He has an interesting, absorbing, unfettered life. He's using the muscles of his brain—strengthening them on some resisting substance. He's in the thick of it.... What fun! Planning, visioning things in his mind, and seeing them take form in the external. He's a builder. He wears an imperturbable mask. That's for defense; but behind it I sometimes see keen, powerful, calculating gleams in his eyes, and I want to know about them, but I can't.... I can't talk to him about any but surface things. I can't show him what is in my heart.... The corsets are between us. He's one of the great powers, and he's mine, a possession like the Kohinoor, but I do not fancy that the Kohinoor constitutes the queen's happiness.

"What are Cresswell and I to each other, anyway? Why, he's my Kohinoor, a possession of great price which endows me with distinction, and runs my credit up into the millions. He's as brilliant and cold and secretive as his prototype. And I—I'm his doll, a very jewel of a doll. One of the prettiest in the world, wonderfully dressed, exquisitely marceled, faultlessly manicured. I can smile enchantingly, and open and shut my mouth to ask for what I want and what I don't want, particularly the latter, and lisp 'thank you' when he drops a diamond necklace or a ruby tiara into my lap.

"I hate a man that puts me on a pedestal. Any woman does. He thinks I'm sugar and salt and will melt and break. I wish he'd come to me, just once, with some enthusiasm and hug me breathless. I'm tired of his everlasting chivalry and deference.... When he begins to treat me with reverence and guards my youth and all that, I'd like to swear at him like the disreputable parrot of a drunken sailor.... Wouldn't I surprise him? I wonder what he would do if I'd cut loose? Oh, dear, I wish he'd come home drunk some night and smash up some of this junk and— what is that phrase of Wallace Martin's—swipe me one; and then be penitent and remorseful and ashamed and human— instead of always being like a darned old statue of the American statesman with one hand thrust in the bosom of his frock-coat.

"I wonder—I wonder—what kind of a husband Eugene would have made. Not one of the amiable, benign, deferential ones, anyway. What were those lines 'Gene used to say?

"'Each life's unfulfilled, you see,And both hang patchy and scrappy.We have not sighed deep, laughed free,Starved, feasted, despaired, been happy!'

"That's it—that's it—that's life. To sigh deep—to laugh free; to make your bed in hell, and then soar on the wings of the morning.... I'm young, beautiful. I have everything but experience. I mean to have it.... No wonder Eve took the apple the serpent offered, if she was as bored in the Garden of Eden as I am. I'd have bitten more than one, though. What is the use of living if you don't live?"

And while Perdita raged in inward rebellion, the world, viewing things from the outside, took an entirely different view of her matter.

Popular opinion inclined to the belief that the good fairies had too heavily dowered this young woman at her cradle, and consequently a readjustment was inevitable, probably by the gracious means of ennobling tribulation. The dramatic event was rather eagerly anticipated. Not that envy had any part in it or that any of Perdita's friends or acquaintances wished to see a fellow being punished for the liberality of Providence. On the contrary. It was merely a sane desire to mark the balances of the universe in faultless equilibrium and to have the comforting assurance that the mills of the gods still ground with the proverbial exactness.

Youth, health, wealth, beauty, happiness, all unlimited! An exasperating spectacle! How could all be right with the world as long as Hebe continued to pour most of the nectar into one glass, while so many thirsty, deserving souls were denied even a sip?

And Perdita went her way and smiled alike on those who caviled and those who applauded. She had accepted her husband's friends as her own with a sort of careless, indifferent good nature and the relations existing between herself and the closely cemented little group were sufficiently harmonious under the circumstances. Maud Carmine and she had struck "leagues of friendship" at once, and Maud's prediction that Hepworth's friends would have to serve as Perdita's relatives would seem to have been verified.

And Maud, through constant association, appeared to have reflected some of Dita's beauty, for there was evidenced the most remarkable change in the plain Miss Carmine, her name no longer prefaced by that deplorable adjective, however.

Alice Wilstead explained it by frankly giving the credit to Perdita. It was she, Alice asserted, who had had the faith and the courage to take Maud vigorously in hand and make of her a new creature as far as the outward presentment was concerned. The results had been so mutually satisfactory as to rivet the friendship between the two; for Dita had proved by her works her belief that there was not the faintest necessity for any such creature as an unattractive woman; and Maud, having lost all faith in the willingness of nature to better her original handiwork, had turned hopefully to art, with the result that she was now one of the most talked-of women in town. By men, because she had recently grown attractive enough for them to discover that she was also extremely agreeable and sympathetic. By women, because they ached to discover her secret. They remembered as easily as the men forgot that for twenty-eight years of her life Maud had been as a weed by the wall, a lank and sallow weed, oppressed by the sparseness of her leaves and the entire absence of either flowers or fruit, and suddenly she had acquired an art, an air, the trick of dress so subtle that it imparted distinction even to her worst points.

But when Perdita proceeded to verify, a little tardily, it is true, the hope of Mrs. Willoughby Hewston, sighingly expressed at the wedding breakfast, and furnished herself with a relative, the coterie gasped. It was not perhaps just the selection Mrs. Hewston would have made for her, but, nevertheless, Perdita had produced a relative, although, it must be confessed, of a rather dubious and indefinite nearness.

If Mrs. Hewston had been questioned on the subject she might have confessed that the relative she had in mind, as presenting an admirable background for a young and lovely girl, was either a silver-haired mother with a white lace cap, and a hair brooch fastening the snowy lawn collar of her black gown; or, in lieu of her, a maiden aunt. Indeed, had Mrs. Hewston been given free choice, she would have inclined toward the latter.

Unquestionably, a maiden aunt is the best possible promoter of that nice sense of the proprieties, those right feelings and carefully graduated moral sentiments which are indispensable to a homeless, penniless young woman scrambling for a living. But Perdita, in presenting her relative, had almost flippantly disregarded these considerations involving a sense of universal fitness. It was a far cry, really an almost revolutionary distance, one felt, from the silver-haired mother or rather acid maiden aunt to Eugene Gresham. Eugene Gresham! Fancy!

For Eugene had returned to his native land with the recognition of Paris and London, even their acclaim—golden bay leaves and purple cloaks. Therefore was he thrice welcomed of New York. Therefore, the next presumption followed as naturally as the first. It was out of the question that Mrs. Hepworth, whose beauty was a matter of international comment, should lack a Gresham portrait, a distinction now unattainable save to those upon the mountain peaks of noble birth, enormous wealth, great achievement, remarkable beauty or superlative notoriety.

As Alice Wilstead pointed out, no one could cavil at any relative Mrs. Hepworth chose to set up, however regretable might be Perdita Carey's claim of kinship with this particular person, and she had certainly, as far as one knew, been discreet enough not to flaunt him during her scrambles. Now, as Mrs. Hepworth's cousin (how many times removed, dear?) he was one more jewel in her crown.

Mrs. Hewston sighingly acquiesced. "Yes, really. As Mrs. Hepworth's relative, yes. But hardly as the guide, philosopher and friend of youth, feminine youth, anyway." Only the happily married might safely claim him, for Gresham, with his fame as a painter of beautiful women and his almost equal reputation as a fascinating person, would not have been commended by any maiden aunt for either right feelings, nice moral sentiments or a discriminating taste for the proprieties.

As for Cresswell Hepworth, he looked after his vast and varied interests, kept up his collections, especially his collection of amulets, in which he was greatly interested, and occupied his leisure in seeing that his wife was sufficiently entertained and amused to gratify the requirements even of her eager youth.

Did she hint a longing for the Roc's egg? It was cabled for within the hour. Did she breathe a desire for the moon? Orders were given that an aëronautic expedition capable of securing it be manned at once.

And yet in spite of all this obvious contentment and happiness, Mr. Willoughby Hewston in the rôle of raven had never ceased to flap his wings and croak. He was particularly in this favorite vein of his one afternoon when he shuffled into his wife's sitting-room, where she and Alice Wilstead sat over their tea-cups. They heard him sighing heavily as he came.

"No, I don't want any tea," he said, letting himself down slowly into an easy chair, "you know I never touch it.

"Poor old Cress!" He shook his head gloomily at a spot in the carpet. "Well, it's just as I predicted. That wife of his is the talk of the town!"

"Oh, my dear!" exclaimed his wife. She, loyal soul, never failed him as audience. A quick glance passed between Mrs. Wilstead and herself, as if he had mentioned the subject uppermost in their minds, and, no doubt, in their conversation.

"Oh, come now, Willoughby," said Alice, instinctively choosing the best method of drawing him out, "you know it's nothing like so bad as that."

Hewston scowled heavily and laid one hand gingerly upon his rheumatic knee, which gave him an especially sharp twinge at the moment. "It's probably worse," he replied with even more than his customary acerbity, "worse than we, any of us, know. Didn't I see them walking up Fifth Avenue together this afternoon, and didn't a fellow speak of it to me? And Cress out of town!"

"Well, let me tell something, dear," said his wife soothingly. "Cress will very soon be in town again, for here are invitations to a dinner the Hepworths are having next week. Quite an informal affair. Perdita writes me, 'Just the little group of Cresswell's best friends, which I hope I may also claim as mine,'" reading from the note she had picked up from the table. "Very sweet of her."

"A dinner, eh," growled Hewston, "with all of us, and I suppose that painter fellow. Well, I only hope it will not fall to me to open poor Cresswell's eyes."

"Oh, Willoughby!"

"I'll not shirk my duty if it does. You can understand that. What evening is this dinner? Next Thursday! Humph! Who is that?" as the curtain before the door was pushed aside and some one entered.

"I!" said Wallace Martin, "only poor little me. They told me to come up. What's happening next Thursday?"

"The Hepworths' dinner. There is probably an invitation awaiting you at home."

"No, there is not," he said. "It's in my pocket now. I picked it up as I was leaving. From what Maud Carmine has just told me, I imagine it's a touching family group composed of ourselves and Eugene Gresham."

"Dear me," deplored Mrs. Hewston, "I do wish she would consider Willoughby more. She must know that he can not endure the sight of Mr. Gresham."

"It is not her fault," said Martin quickly, "as far as I can make out from what Maud told me. Cress became imbued with the idea that he wanted his dear old friends clustering about the board, and made out the list himself."

"How like a man!" remarked Alice Wilstead gloomily. "But why, just now?"

"Oh, he's been adding to that pet collection of amulets of his, and he wanted to show us his new acquisitions. That's the root of it, I fancy. I don't imagine the lovely Perdita pined for us. She has been a creature of moods lately. Very hotty-like with me."

"She was actually almost impertinent to Willoughby the other day." Mrs. Hewston spoke with a hushed mournfulness. "I'm afraid all this luxury and adulation has turned her head, and Willoughby spoke so gently to her, too, did you not, dear?"

"Ugh! Humph!" quoth Willoughby.

CHAPTER IV

OUR LOVING FRIENDS

AS it chanced the Hepworths were not particularly fortunate in their choice of an evening for the dinner so gloomily anticipated by their guests. The weather was unpropitious. All day rain had threatened, and the air had been almost sultry, a parting word flung over her shoulder to autumn by a mischievous July who should long ago have vanished. As the evening wore on clouds banked more densely upon the horizon, occasionally muttering thunder, and this electric hint of storm in the air had in some way communicated itself to the mental atmosphere. A sense of foreboding, a consciousness of discord, seemed to swell ominously now and again beneath the smooth and colorful surface of the dinner. Even the dullest of the guests felt that, and to the intuitive, the stately progress of the meal was nerve-racking.

When the hostess rose, every individual sigh of relief involuntarily exhaled became a chorus, shocking in volume.

They winced nervously, but in spite of it, each guest stood by his guns. They had, apparently with one mind, and certainly with one voice, decided against bridge. The ordeal of dinner bravely borne, licensed them, they felt, even bestowed the accolade of privilege on them, to escape the prevalent atmosphere of unrest as quickly as possible.

In the brief time they had allotted themselves to remain, barely skirting the limits of conventional decency, Alice Wilstead, Isabel and Willoughby Hewston and Wallace Martin had elected to take their coffee and cigarettes on a small balcony opening from the drawing-room by long French windows and giving upon a garden, quite half of a city block, with thick, close-cropped lawn, and black masses of dense shrubbery permeating the damp and sultry air with the mingled fragrance of earth and leaves and some late-blooming flowers. Maud Carmine, good-natured as usual, had seated herself at the piano, across the length of the room from the balcony, to play a ballad of Chaminade's at her host's request.

Hepworth, who alone appeared to be oblivious of the sinister atmospheric influences, leaned his elbows on the piano and listened, occasionally unhesitatingly breaking the flow of the music with conversation.

With their friend and host thus comfortably within sight, yet out of earshot, the group on the balcony felt at liberty to speak with freedom; no danger of sudden appearances, consequent jumps and hot wonder at what might have been overheard.

"Gad!" said Mr. Hewston, more gray and pink, puffy and heavily financial than ever, "when will people learn to eat and drink without flowers on the table?"

"No flowers!" repeated Alice Wilstead. "It would look dull, would it not?" From her tone it was evident that she had paid little heed to his words.

"What difference does that make?" he argued irritably. "You don't go to dinner to look at the table decorations. But if they must have 'em, why can't they have the artificial kind or those paper things. Anything but the beastly, smelly, live ones."

"Don't you really care for them?" she asked, laughing. "I thought every one loved flowers. To tell the truth, they were about all that made that unending dinner bearable to me. They were so exquisitely arranged."

"Oh, that," in grudging admission, "goes without saying in this house, but," fretfully, "they were all the loud smelling kind."

"She always arranges them herself," said Mrs. Wilstead, "she has wonderful taste, wonderful. Her house, her clothes, even down to the smallest detail of the table. Marvelous!"

"Humph! she doesn't show the same taste in men," grunted Hewston. "No brains at all."

Mrs. Wilstead leaned forward to tap his arm with her fan.

"Do not make any mistake on that score," her voice was emphatic, "she has plenty of brains."

"Humph!" more scornfully than before. "Then I wish they'd keep her from making the fool of herself that she is doing now."

"Hs-s-sh," Alice looked as if she would like to thrust a handkerchief into his mouth. "Ah!" glancing up with relief as Isabel and Wallace Martin turned from their contemplation of the garden over the balcony railing. "Sit down here," she motioned to two chairs beside her.

"Dear me, Alice," said Martin, "isn't your face tired with the effort of keeping the corners of your mouth turned up and the sparkle in your eyes? The only person who seems calm and serene this evening is dear old Hepworth. What do you think it is on his part, the quintessence of pose or simple, uncomprehending, fatuous ignorance?"

"My God!" growled Hewston explosively. His wife started nervously.

"Oh Willoughby dear, not so loud! Wallace," in what was as near a tone of reproof as she could achieve, "I do wish you wouldn't say those reckless things before Willoughby. You know how emotional he is."

Alice also shook her head impatiently. "Don't you think we are a lot of old gossips magnifying matters enormously? You may expect so beautiful a young woman as Dita Hepworth to be more or less talked about; but there is probably a perfect understanding between herself and Cress. Lord help her if there isn't," she added almost under her breath, "I've known him many a year."

"'When an old bachelor marries a young wife, what is he to expect?'" quoted Martin impressively. As a would-be playwright he had the dramatists at his finger-tips.

"Wallace, you are too bad," expostulated Mrs. Wilstead. "No wonder you quote from *The School for Scandal*. Here we are a lot of old wreckers doing our best to shatter a reputation. Why Dita Hepworth and Eugene Gresham have known each other ever since they were children. Naturally, she shows her pleasure in his society."

"Oh pish!" scoffed Wallace Martin, "those unconcealed glances she bestowed on him at dinner spoke not of sisterly affection, and how we all squirmed under them and wondered miserably if Hepworth was seeing them too."

"He always did see everything without appearing to," murmured Mrs. Wilstead gloomily.

"Now merely as a sporting chance, which would you bet on," said Martin, drawing his chair a bit nearer, "the rich, middle-aged husband, or the fascinating artist, the painter of beautiful women, in the zenith of his fame? It is the same old plot you know, and the oft-told tale may have just two endings. First, she goes off with the artist, lives a squalid and miserable life abroad, falls ill, and dies, holding the hand and imploring the forgiveness of her husband, who conveniently and miraculously appears. In the second ending, she makes all preparations to flee and then something occurs which causes her to see the sculpturesque nobility of her husband's character and the curtain descends to slow sweet music while they stand heart to heart in the calcium light of a grand reconciliation scene."

"Oh, Wallace, do forget for once that you are trying to be a playwright. Forget the shop." Mrs. Wilstead was irritable. "I do wish she would join us," looking about her nervously, "I want to go home. Is she utterly careless?"

"Only absorbed," returned Martin calmly. "Didn't you hear her ask him before they left the room, to come and look at the picture gallery where he is to paint her portrait? She wanted him to judge of the lighting—a night like this. I thought I saw the flutter of her white gown in the garden yonder a bit ago."

"Oh do, for goodness sake, change the subject," said Alice Wilstead hurriedly. "I am sure Cresswell must think it queer the way we are all sitting out here with our heads together, in the teeth of that approaching storm."

"Not at all," Martin reassured her. "Don't you see that Maud is doing her duty heroically? Maud isn't the wife's confidante and dearest friend for nothing."

"Isn't it perfectly wonderful about Maud?" commented Mrs. Hewston. "You all know what a plain, angular creature she was, nothing really to recommend her but her music and she always spoiled that by playing with her shoulder blades."

"She's an extremely stunning woman," said Wallace Martin shortly.

"And all due to Dita Hepworth," announced Mrs. Wilstead. "Wonderful! I never saw a woman with such a genius for dress and decoration. If her beauty wasn't such an obvious quality, I should think it was due to her almost uncanny knowledge of what is becoming and—Ah, thank Heaven, here she is!"

CHAPTER V

PERDITA'S TALISMAN

Perdita Hepworth had entered the room, with Eugene Gresham just a step or two behind her, and, after a glance in the direction of Maud Carmine and her husband, had moved toward the little group on the balcony. Gresham was used to any amount of attention and admiration, but the adulatory interest which he may have merited and had, in fact, grown to regard as his due, was always conspicuously lacking when he appeared with Perdita.

"The picture gallery is the chosen spot," she announced as if bearing some intelligence for which they had long been waiting, "and the sittings are to be begun at once. I remember when I first knew Maud Carmine, she said to me, 'Fancy what it must be like to have your portrait painted by Eugene Gresham!'" Her low laughter rang with a sort of triumphant amusement. "'Dear child,' I answered, 'I have had my portrait painted by him so many times that there would be no novelty whatever in the experience.' You know," to Mrs. Hewston, who looked faintly puzzled, "'Gene and I have always known each other." She looked over at Gresham who was seated on the arm of a chair talking to Maud Carmine and Hepworth. "Has Maud been playing for Cresswell?" she asked suddenly. "He is so fond of her music."

"Yes, she has been playing delightfully," answered Mrs. Wilstead, "and she looks charming to-night. Maud who was always regarded as an ugly duckling has suddenly become a swan."

"Ah, why not?" said Perdita carelessly. "Maud hadn't the faintest idea how to make the most of herself. She gave the effect of hard lines and angles, and hair and eyes and skin all cut from the same piece, a dingy dust color. Like every other woman of that type she has a perfect passion for mustard colors and hard grays. Ugh!" she shivered. "The only thing to do with Maud was to make her realize that she must look odd and mysterious, you know. That was all. Oh, she is beckoning to me. They want something."

She crossed the room with that grace of bearing which nature had bestowed upon her and with the added poise and assurance gained within the last two years. She still gave the effect of extreme simplicity in dress but it was retained as by a miracle, for although she wore no jewels her white gown was of the most exquisite and costly lace. But her head was undeniably carried a trifle higher than usual, and a very close observer might have read boredom in her eyes, defiance in her chin, rebellion in her shoulders. As she turned from the little group on the balcony, she bit her lip irritably, before she again composed her features to the conventional smile of hostess-like cordiality.

Alice Wilstead followed her with puzzled eyes.

"It is very difficult to understand a beauty," she said plaintively to Martin.

"Put it more correctly," as he blew a cloud of smoke. "Say, it's difficult to understand a woman."

"But I do not find it so," she smiled. "I'm one myself. I'm on to all our various vagaries, but Dita Hepworth puzzles me. Look at this house. There are effects here in decoration, so beautiful and unusual that every one says Eugene Gresham directed them. I know he did not. Look at Maud Carmine, and yet Dita herself usually wears the plainest of gowns."

"I must confess," said Martin, "that I do not follow you."

45

"Perhaps not," she mused, then with more animation. "Come, Wallace, tell me exactly how she impresses you."

"That is easy," he replied. "She is one of the prettiest women I ever saw in my life."

"Ah, of course," in annoyance, "but I didn't mean that. That is no impression of character."

"Mm," he pondered. "It isn't much of one, no."

Alice leaned back in her chair. "I seem to discern depths in her that the rest of you refuse to see. You stop at her beauty and are content with never a peep beneath the surface."

Martin tossed his cigarette over the railing into the garden. "Frankly, I think that you are searching for something that isn't there," he said abruptly. "The gods never bestow all their gifts on one person. Since you profess to know your own self so well you should realize that women so very pretty as Mrs. Hepworth are rarely clever. Why should they be? It is enough of an excuse for existence that they are beautiful."

"It is indeed," growled Hewston, who had been absorbed in sulky meditation for some time. "I'd be contented if I thought she had enough head on her shoulders to keep straight and not involve good old Hepworth in God knows what."

Wallace laughed. "I'll lay you a wager, Mrs. Wilstead," he whispered, tapping her fan with his finger-tips, "that the way things are going now there will be a split in the Hepworth household within three months."

"Do not say it," she cried quickly. "I can not bear to think of such a thing."

"I'll give you heavy odds, too," he went on cynically, leaning forward to regard the group at the piano. "I'll make it a bracelet against a box of cigars, provided I'm allowed to choose the brand of cigars."

"You might as well put in another provision then," she retorted, "provided I am allowed to choose the bracelet. My taste in ornaments, dear Wallace, is both unique and expensive. I like only odd jewelry."

"Odd jewelry! That is an old fad of yours, Alice," said Hepworth's voice behind her.

She started slightly, she had not noticed his approach. "And your own," she smiled up at him. "Have you secured any new amulets lately, Cresswell?"

"Yes, one. It is a beauty, a scarab. I must show it to you; also another, a carved bloodstone set in very curiously wrought iron. I got that from a Gipsy woman. It is an old Romany talisman."

"Do let us see them," pleaded Mrs. Hewston.

"Certainly, I shall be delighted to. Excuse me a few moments. I will get the box myself. Naturally I would not trust it to the servants." He smiled at his weakness.

"Naturally," said Hewston. "Come, let us all get into the drawing-room to look at them. It is beginning to rain anyway."

It was only a few moments before Hepworth returned bearing a large, black leather box. He placed it on a table just under the light and then choosing a key from a ring, fitted it into the lock.

47

"I hold one key," he said to the group pressing about him as he lifted the lid, "and Perdita the other. That is in case she may want to wear any of these trinkets."

Alice Wilstead had been looking at Mrs. Hepworth at the moment her husband entered the room and she alone had noticed that Dita started violently when her eyes had fallen on the box and that all the rich color had fled her cheek, leaving her, for a second or two, white as a ghost.

The box held a series of trays, each padded and velvet lined and upon these were fastened Cresswell Hepworth's noted collection of amulets. Most of these talismans were very ancient, many of them revealed the most beautiful workmanship. All of them were distinctive. Each one, almost without exception, had a history, strange, romantic or sinister, and these were all duly catalogued, but it was never necessary for Hepworth to refer to this written history. He had not only the symbolic significance of his favorite toys, but also the vicissitudes through which they had passed, at his finger ends.

The top trays held scarabs, one of the most remarkable collections of them extant, commemorating certain mighty and fallen dynasties; or this reign or that of remote Egyptian rulers long crumbled to dust, and Hepworth lifted them lovingly from their trays and turning them deftly in his fingers explained their histories and expatiated on their beauty.

Beneath the scarabs lay the jade talismans exquisitely carved and handed down from distant centuries. The hearts that had once beat beneath them had long been dust, but the talismans, with no stain of time upon them to dim their luster, would still serve as emblems of good luck to future generations. Then there were quaint amber charms preserving the warmth and flooding radiance of the sunlight that sparkles on sea foam in their depths, and opals delicately clouded with mystery, their

48

"hearts of fire bedreamed in haze," carbuncles, jasper and hyacinth, all in their time the almost priceless possessions of their owners because of the mystic significance attaching to them. And then there were trays containing a somewhat heterogeneous collection of old pieces of beaten silver and iron with odd characters on them, representing periods of even greater antiquity than scarab or jade.

These amulets were in many instances the memorials of bitter feuds and hot duels, fought on the moment, at the gleam of a talisman which both contestants claimed. More than one had been hastily rifled from the dead, and more than one had been bestowed by a great lady on an untitled lover of empty purse to aid him in winning fame and fortune.

"By the way, Alice," said Hepworth suddenly, "you have seen Dita's amulet, have you not? It is almost, if not quite the gem of the collection."

"No, I have never seen it," Mrs. Wilstead's whole piquant face was alive with interest. "But I have heard of it. It was through it that you met, was it not?"

Dita nodded. The color had come back to her face. "It was that old talisman he was really interested in," she said. "I always tell him he married me to get it."

Hepworth laughed. "It is well worth any one's interest. It has been in her family for generations, and there are all sorts of legends and traditions connected with it. It is said to give his heart's desire to whomever possesses it, isn't it, Dita?"

"More than that," she replied, a little strangely, or at least so it seemed to Alice Wilstead. "He to whom it is given—and it can not be bought or bartered, it must always be bestowed—must sooner or later reveal himself in his true character, either his baseness or his nobility."

"Fascinating!" cried the women in chorus. "What is it like?"

"It is a square of crystal set in silver and gold. About the silver is twined one of those old Celtic chains which can only be seen with a microscope, where the links are so tiny that we have no instruments delicate enough to fasten them together and which were believed to have been made by the fairies. And now for a sight of it."

He was about to lift the next tray, when Dita laid a detaining hand on his arm. "It isn't there, Cresswell," she said in a quick, low voice.

As if he had not heard her or had not taken in the full import of her words, he laid the tray carefully upon the table, disclosing the one beneath. Like the others, it too was full of curious amulets, but one space was empty. Perdita's talisman was indeed missing.

"Why, Dita!" he exclaimed. "You did not mention to me—"

She shot a quick, unmistakable glance at Gresham. "Didn't I?" she interrupted before he could go further. "It's being mended."

"Ah, those antique bits, they are always coming to pieces, at least I know mine are," said Mrs. Wilstead with hasty fluency. "But, Cresswell, there is still another tray, and I must see its contents before I go home.""Make it a month," said Martin in her ear. "I said three, didn't I?"

CHAPTER VI

50

SIROCCO

"Good night, Hewston, good night, Alice. Don't go yet, Gresham." Hepworth laid a detaining hand on the artist's arm. "Sit down and smoke. We haven't had a moment to discuss this portrait matter yet."

"I think," said Dita, moving toward the door, "that I shall leave you two to discuss it and go to bed."

"Oh, my dear," her husband detained her with the same light touch with which he had held Gresham. He pushed an easy chair forward so that she should be seated between Eugene and himself. "We are going to get all the details of the portrait settled to-night. A portrait of you and painted by Gresham is sure to bloom and be admired for a century or two at any rate."

Dita looked at him quickly as if suspecting him of some intention beyond the discussion of the contemplated portrait, but meeting the smiling blankness of his expression, turned away, not in the least reassured, but more puzzled than ever, and sinking listlessly into the chair sat staring moodily before her with veiled eyes and compressed lips.

Eugene glanced at her uneasily, a frown between his brows. He knew her like a book. She had always, always from childhood, been a creature of moods. He was perfectly familiar with the various stages of the sirocco, as he had long ago named her outbursts. She would become restless, abstracted, absent, and then she would sit and brood as she was doing now, until finally the sullen and threatening atmosphere would be cleared by a burst of storm, a swift cyclone of anger.

Gresham gave the faintest of sighs and an almost imperceptible shrug of the shoulders. This was a situation which he foresaw would require all his tact and ingenuity.

"Is the picture gallery all right? Did you find it satisfactory?" asked Hepworth.

"Excellent!" Eugene's brow cleared. He spoke with enthusiasm. "Yes, I told Perdita that the lighting there will be perfect. I've about decided to paint her in white. Yes," scrutinizing the indifferent object of the discussion narrowly and yet remotely, as if he were visualizing his finished portrait of her, "white velvet, I think, and rather a blare of jewels. You see I want to bring out the dominating quality of her beauty, harp on it, you know, so I want to present her eclipsing and reducing to their proper places all the splendid accessories with which we can surround her."

Her husband nodded approvingly. "What do you think, Dita?"

"Oh, by all means," she roused herself to answer, but making no effort to conceal the irony of her tones. "Let Eugene give me all the distinction and grace he is noted for bestowing on, you observe I do not say perceiving in, his clients, or patients, or patrons, whatever he may call them. Make the stones of my tiara and necklace even bigger and whiter and more sparkling than they are, Eugene. Or better still, I'll wear my diamond collar and my string of rubies and my rope of sapphires, all shouting hurrah at once, three cheers for the red, white and blue! Make me all glittery, Eugene, throw my sables over my shoulders."

"By Jove!" cried Gresham, interrupting her, a white flash of enthusiasm across his face, "you may not dream it, Dita, but that's it exactly. You've hit it."

"Yes," she went on satirically, "and present me in the middle of all this splendor, overcome by the 'burden of an honor into which I was not born.'"

"But you were born to it," interposed her husband quickly, "no one more so."

"Perhaps," she sighed a little, her eyes and voice grew softer, "but at a time when the outward manifestation had vanished."

The glow had lingered, even become intensified in Gresham's face. "By Jove!" he cried again, "you were trying to be sarcastic and all that, Dita, but it was a great idea of yours just the same. I will paint your portrait and it shall be hung side by side with my working girl. They shall be companions of contrast. You see," explaining his idea to Hepworth, "I am going to paint my working girl in the city streets just at twilight on a winter evening, hastening home after the day's long toil. The lights and colors of the shop windows dance and glitter about her, blurred by the falling snow. Everything, lights, buildings, passers-by, are all in that blurred, indistinct atmosphere, and she, herself, is a part of the blur, looking through it, with her young, worn face and wistful eyes, craving the beauty and the joy of life."

"No, no!" cried Dita suddenly. Rising, she moved rapidly up and down the room, her head bent, her finger at her lip. "No!" she cried again, her voice deeply vibrating. "I reckon you've just missed it, Eugene, it's too—too conventional. I can imagine something truer than that. My working girl, if I were painting her, should not be born to toil, not always have regarded it as the great fact of existence, an inevitable portion of her days and years from which she has never dreamed of escape. No, I would picture her delicate, highly nurtured, with traditions of race and breeding behind her; but poor, oh, very poor. And she shouldn't look out on life with resigned, wistful eyes, but with passionate, demanding ones, rebelling that her youth, her wonderful, beautiful, dreaming youth was passing in a tomb of tradition, a green and flowery tomb perhaps, maybe an old southern garden, but nevertheless a place of dead lives, dead memories, dead customs. And she, this girl, hates it, the dust and must of it. She hears always in her ears the surges of that mighty ocean of life. And she can't resist it. She can't. Then because her heart is set on it, she comes to a great city like this, comes with all her high hopes and her untarnished confidence in herself; and all this magnificent swirling tide of life, with its mingled and mingling streams, seems to bear her onward to the highest crest of the highest wave. Then she begins to hear, at first faintly and then ever louder and more menacing, the voice of New York, with its ceaseless reiteration of one theme, 'pay, pay, pay.' She turns desperately to her little accomplishments, those little, untrained, unskilful things that she can do, straws on that ocean; and expects them to save her.

"Ah!" she drew her hand across her brow, her face contracting a moment. "Then comes the grind between the millstones, the continual disappointments, the terror by day and night, the rent, that rolls like a snowball, the dreary evenings which she must spend alone in the dreary little room, while all the time she hears the mocking invitation of the great, glittering city to partake of her many feasts.

"And she," again Dita sighed deeply, "she begins to believe herself doomed to dash her youth and beauty against the walls of a tomb. And she has to learn so many things, among them the hideous accomplishment of making both ends meet. What does she know of the use and value of money? Oh, of course all kinds of cheap, left-handed pleasures are offered her, because people consider her pretty, but it is an impossibility for her to accept them. She has been born in the traditions of real lace and real jewels. And the panic-fear! Ah!—" she broke off abruptly.

"Dear me, Dita. You should have been an orator." For the past five minutes Eugene had been scarcely able to conceal his irritation, frowning, biting his lips, twisting in his chair and casting furtive glances at Hepworth. "I remember you used to be given to those bursts of eloquence now and then."

"And what finally becomes of her?" asked Hepworth of his wife, ignoring Eugene's interruption. His voice was low, expressing nothing more than a polite interest.

"I don't know," said Dita wearily. "A number of things. She may comfortably die, or marry, poor thing, any one who will have her."

"Very dramatic," said Gresham dryly. "You always did have histrionic talent, Dita. I've often wondered that you did not attempt the stage."

Perdita opened and closed her eyes once or twice as if she had just returned from a far country.

"I certainly wasn't much of a success at painting lamp-shades and menus, was I, Eugene, in spite of your early training?"

He shrugged his shoulders without answering, made a slight, disclaiming gesture with one hand and rose to his feet. "What!" listening intently as a clock chimed somewhere. "I had no idea it was so late." His face cleared. He was evidently relieved at his chance of escape. He shook hands with Hepworth and then turned to Dita. "Remember that the first sitting will be at twelve o'clock Wednesday morning, and please don't keep me waiting. That is a fact that I have to impress on these charming women," he turned laughingly to Hepworth, "that I am neither their manicure nor hair-dresser. I am accustomed to keep them waiting if I choose."

"I'll be ready," she said indifferently, but Eugene noticed with apprehension, even alarm, that those deep vibrations which spoke of barely controlled emotion were still existent in her tones. "I'll be ready, velvet, diamonds, hurrah of jewels, if you wish, sables and all."

Again a gust of wind swept through the room and Hepworth went over to close a window.

Eugene took quick advantage of the occasion. "For Heaven's sake," he whispered, "pull yourself together."

His words were too late. Too late by half an hour. The sirocco had done its work.

CHAPTER VII

THE GIFT OF FREEDOM

With the departure of a third person the situation immediately changed complexion. It became more intimate and therefore more embarrassing. With Eugene had departed the audience and the stimulus of playing to it. The star and the stage manager were left alone. Untrammeled emotional expression no longer seemed an heroic necessity. Under the calm, unreadable, steady regard of her husband's eyes it held its elements of banality and of sensationalism, of pseudo-emotion. Dita became sullen. "I think I shall go to bed," she said abruptly and for the second time and then turned to the door.

"Wait a moment." His voice was courteous, pleasant, but it would have been a dull ear which could not have discerned the tone of command beneath its even modulations.

It was new to Dita and arresting, and she paused, wavered a moment and came back to the chair she had left and folding her arms upon its high cushioned back, stood with still, sullen mouth and downcast eyes, exhaling reluctance. She was feeling the reaction from her late mood of exaltation, of dramatic visioning of poignant past experiences.

He waited a second or so, and then said, "Your working girl was a far more dramatic conception than Gresham's. It might not lend itself so much to pictorial representation. It might be more literary." He appeared to give this question some consideration. "However," he dismissed it with a wave of the hand, "that is neither here nor there. What counts is this, were you the girl whose life you described so feelingly and dramatically?"

There was silence between them for a moment. Dita's first impulse was to maintain it indefinitely; ignore this question with barely suggested contempt; with a faint gesture of dissent, signify that she considered it a crudity, almost a vulgarity, and lightly, languidly, indifferently dismiss the whole subject and leave the room. She knew how, intuitively. Behind her were generations who understood how to flick an unpleasant situation from the tips of their fingers, who would ignore and dismiss with amused disdain an invitation to exculpate themselves or explain, when to explain meant practically to retract. But false as she felt, with waves of shame, she had been to her traditions and upbringing in revealing her emotion, she was no coward. She lifted her head and met his eyes. Gray eyes faced gray eyes—but with a difference. Hers were the passionate, emotional Irish gray—with black beneath them, and the long curling black lashes, but his were like mountain lakes, reflecting a gray and steely sky. Hers revealed all the secrets she might wish to hide; his concealed all his secrets admirably—discreet windows, revealing nothing but what their owner desired they should reveal.

"Yes," she said with defiant brevity.

He appeared again to give this reply due consideration. He had risen now and was walking up and down the floor. "What an impression it must have made on you!" he said at last, very gently.

She plaited the lace of her sleeve. "You knew about me before we were married," she said. "Why—?"

"Quite true, but sometimes something is said, it may be only a word, and one's eyes become, as it were, unsealed. One sees a perfectly familiar object or situation in an entirely new light. Your attitude now," he turned to her rather sharply, "is that I am about to blame you, to take you to task. Far from it. Why should I blame you for what has been beyond your power? Your words to-night have made me realize that it has been quite impossible for you to care for me, and that I have not been able to make you happy. Ah," lifting his hand as she was about to speak, "do not disclaim it. I know. You see, that very fact sends the whole house of cards tumbling. The bitterness with which you have spoken to-night would not have been in your mind, rankling, rankling all this time, if you had been a happy woman. It was bound to burst into flame sooner or later."

"Oh!" she broke out. "You have always won. You do not know what it is like to lose; but I—I missed every mark I aimed at. I came up from the South, so dead sure that I was a very gifted and accomplished person, and that all I had to do was to hold out my apron and all the beautiful and delightful things would tumble into it. But this great city surely taught me a lesson, and she's no very gentle teacher, either. And I used to sit up there in that tiresome little apartment among those candle-shades and cotillion favors and think how—how pretty I was," she flushed under his smile, "and rage, and get sick with disgust when I thought how I would look after about twenty years of that kind of life. I knew exactly how I'd look. I'd be one of those peaked, wistful-eyed old maids, with rusty black clothes turning green and brown, and a general air of apology for living. I could just see myself ironing out the ribbons of my winter bonnet with which to trim my summer hat, and then laundering my handkerchiefs and pasting them on the window-panes to dry. And life, life was like a great, wonderful river, flowing by and leaving me stranded on the shore. And then you came."

Hepworth laughed. "I don't wonder that you took the alternative. I'm conceited enough to think it better than those ugly pictures your young eyes were gazing at."

"Yes, they were ugly," she agreed. "Life just seemed like a dark, dreary, cobwebby passageway, but I always felt as if I might come to a door any minute and step through it into a beautiful garden. You seemed the door." She spoke the last words a little shyly.

He glanced at her again, inscrutable, unfathomable things in that gaze. "Ah, youth, youth and the waste of it!" There were tones in his voice that brought the tears to her eyes, but he did not see them. He was musing on the accident of her life, this flower of the dust, which he had taken from the dingy environment she loathed. He had lavished all the beauty and experience within his power upon her, and taken away perhaps the one thing that had redeemed her life. He had seen only the limitations and the makeshifts and how they had oppressed her dainty and fastidious spirit; but it had never struck him before that in lifting her away from them, above them, he had taken from her the one thing that might have glorified her life, that the sordidness and the scrimpiness were for her for ever haunted by the unexpected. That because she was young and beautiful and free, the dreariness must have been irradiated always by the rainbow tints of romance; and he had given her all the beauty and glitter his money could buy in exchange for the joy of a dream, and fancied that he had actually done something for her.

"Dita, forgive me," he murmured, a curiously bitter smile about his mouth.

"Forgive you!" she looked at him a little cautiously. She didn't understand the workings of his mind. He never gave her a hint either in eyes or expression that would seem as a clue for her to follow.

"Yes. You should." Again he smiled at her. "You didn't get a fair exchange. I see that very plainly now."

"You must not speak like that," she said quickly. "Believe me, it was a great deal more than a fair exchange and I have always regarded it so. Why do you think I have not been happy?"

"Because you have never really loved me."

"But I—I have always liked you," she cried quickly. "But," forlornly, "you knew the truth at the time. Even if I had not, I should have had to marry you anyway. I was so deep in debt I couldn't help it. I could not manage any more than I can speak Sanscrit. So you see that there is nothing to forgive. Believe me, I am always grateful, for before I married you, I thought and thought, but I could see no other way."

He laughed again. He couldn't help it. He had a sense of humor and he seemed to see, in a flashlight of vision, shocked Romance gather up her skirts and shake the dust of Dita's threshold from her winged shoes.

"You are so really fearless and honest, Dita, that I venture to ask the question." He put it with a rather diffident gentleness. "You have found it quite impossible to care for me?"

"Oh, no," impulsively. "I have always liked you. I am really very fond of you. But I am always tongue-tied before you. I never can think of anything to say to you and I always say foolish things." She regarded him with a wistful timidity.

He laughed ruefully. It was sorry mirth. "That is a proof of my stupidity, my child, not yours."

He opened his mouth to speak, then closed it again. Up and down the room he walked twice, three times, engrossed. Then having arrived at a decision, he put it into words. "Dita," he stopped before her and looked at her earnestly, "perhaps I am utterly rash and foolish, but will you answer me one question?

61

But first get all melodramatic ideas of the state of my feelings out of your head." His smile was faintly cynical, obscurely so. "And believe me, that what really concerns me is your happiness. Are you in love with Eugene Gresham?"

She started, cast one quick glance at him, and then stared frowningly before her, but he noticed that her hand trembled on the back of the chair. "Why do you ask me that? I—I am married to you—I—" her voice faltered, broke.

"Oh, no conventional utterances, please," he cried quickly. "That is not worthy of you, not like you. There should be, there must be absolute sincerity between us now. Tell me, Perdita, are you in love with Eugene Gresham?"

"Ah, that I do not know." She looked beyond him and, still gazing, shook her head. "I do not know. I never have known, never been sure. We were boy and girl together, he a few years older. He is associated in my mind with the life of green old gardens and the smell of jasmine flowers. He lives in a wonderful world, a world of color that something in me always yearns toward. It seems to me sometimes as if I would rise to it, and my heart would blossom in purple and red. I seem doomed to talk foolishly to you," she exclaimed rather piteously, "but most people's hidden thoughts would sound foolish to others, would they not?"

"Go on, my dear." Then his controlled utterance gave way. "For heaven's sake, why should you not feel that you can say anything to me? What kind of an idea have I given you of myself? But tell me," quickly subduing his emotion, "what is it you feel?"

"As if—as if my heart were a flower which had never really bloomed—a cold, tightly folded bud, that yet held within the colorless outer leaves wonderful red and purple petals. All there, awaiting a sesame, and I sometimes dream that only Eugene can give me that sesame. But," the glow left her eyes, her head drooped, "I don't know, I don't know. I thought I was sure once that I loved him. I do not know now."

"Where was Gresham during the time you were struggling here?" he asked presently. And it struck her irrelevantly.

"In the East somewhere, I think. Doing his desert pictures. I used to hear from him once in a great while."

He said nothing. Then he came nearer and took both her hands in his.

"Dita, my clear, I'm going to be egotistical and talk about myself for a minute. Let me see if I can explain." Again that worn and flashing smile, with a deeper touch of cynicism, flitted over his arrogant face.

"'King Canute was weary-hearted,He had reigned for years a score,Pushing, struggling, battling, fighting,Killing much and robbing more.'

"Let us hope that it is not quite so bad as the last line infers; but it gives the idea, the picture. Well, Dita, I saw you, a beautiful flower, purple and red, if you will, although I do not think the combination of colors appropriate. And you were blooming in a tin can in a tenement window. It was insupportable, so I dreamed of transplanting the flower into its fitting surroundings, a marble court. That was what I crudely thought would mean your happiness. But I never secured the flower to adorn the marble court. Believe that. Above all, I wanted and I want its happiness. Dita, I'm weary-hearted, but I long—I long above all things—to make you happy. Take the poor surroundings that I can give you; but let your beauty have its meed, let your heart flower as it will. Feel free to meet, with outstretched hands, the romance your youth has dreamed of, for, Dita, I, who have only fettered you with jewels, am going to give you something really worth while, thanking God very humbly that it is in my power to do so, and the gift is freedom. You are free from now on."

She started back, looking at him in frowning bewilderment and yet he saw deep within her eyes a wild gleam of hope, of joy. "Free!" she repeated uncertainly, "Free! How can I be free when I am married to you?"

"Free! How can I be free?"

He laughed once more, and the dreariness of that laughter rang suddenly hours afterward in her ears. "Those things can always be arranged," he said. "But I am going to ask you a favor." Although he said "favor" her quick ear caught the ring of authority in his tone. "Since you are not sure that you love Gresham, I am going to ask that you wait a year before securing your legal freedom. You shall have it, whether you decide on him or not. Oh, believe that. Ah, one more request. Let me urge you not to have your portrait painted just now. In view of possible future events, it is much wiser, much safer to let that go for the present. I think you will have to trust my judgment here. There is no danger of your beauty waning." Again his worn and flashing smile. "And now, it is very late and I think you had better get some sleep. Good night." He smiled again, but she noticed how dreadfully tired he looked. She winced a bit in soul.

"I am sorry that it has been such a fizzle," she turned to him with a sort of shy, girlish friendliness and impulsiveness.

He smiled again and lightly touched her cheek with his finger. "Give no more thought to that." He turned abruptly away.

"Ah, Dita," his voice arrested her from the threshold, "one more request I am going to make and that is that you get your amulet to-morrow. If not I shall have to see about it myself and I am really too busy to bother with it at present." Again that iron ring of authority was in his voice, but authority masked in velvet. "Will you very kindly attend to this, my dear?"

She nodded mutely from the doorway, but did not lift her down-bent head, nor raise her eyes to his.

CHAPTER VIII

FOOLS' LAUGHTER

When Dita wakened the next morning, it was very late, almost noon. She came slowly to waking consciousness over wastes of apprehension, oppressed by some heavy sense of disaster. What had happened? Ah, she remembered it, it was last night. She squirmed uncomfortably and then lay gazing with somber and introspective eyes about the beautiful room. Slowly, the chaotic and uncomfortable thoughts which thronged confusingly in her mind resolved themselves into two or three distinct facts as scorching to her sensitiveness as if written in letters of fire. First, she had let herself go unwarrantably. An electric storm always exerted a sinister effect upon her, inducing a wildness, a recklessness at first, eventually followed by melancholy and culminating either in tears or temper. And she had yielded weakly to every phase of this storm-induced mood.

Why did events have to take the bits in their teeth and gallop madly along the road to ruin at the most placid and unexpected moments? Why should an electric storm have blotted the sky and flashed its jagged lightning over her nerves that especial evening? Why had she not mastered the sirocco, driven it off in its first stealthy approaches? But she melted to self-pity; Cresswell should not have taken her so seriously. He might have realized that the storm, and that tiresome dinner, and those tiresome people had goaded her unendurably. Grant them every virtue, every grace, admit that there might have been an attraction between herself and them in ordinary circumstances, but the fact that they were old friends of her husband changed the whole chemical situation. Attraction became repulsion, attempt to conceal the fact as she would. But self-pity ultimately merged into self-accusation. No matter what the causes, she had made a melodramatic scene. She had told a lot of bare truths, which, like all bare truths, were only half truths; about Eugene, for instance, practically admitting that she loved him.

Well, did she? She sat up suddenly in bed and pushed the hair back from her brow with both hands. She pondered intensely a moment. She didn't know. She really didn't know. Was it love, this feeling she had for him, had had for him ever since she had been a girl of fifteen? It was a powerful attraction anyway—a sympathy, an understanding.

And Cresswell had offered her freedom, freedom! What did it mean? Her heart began to beat quickly, excitedly. It meant the great adventure ... if one had the courage ... one need "mourn no joy untasted, envy no bliss gone by." She would throw off this ennui, this apathy which afflicted her. She was free, free to seek and meet the unexpected. The great adventure, a thousand adventures were before her. At last, she would live. Suddenly she remembered her amulet. She must get it. She gave this a moment's consideration, and then, before summoning her maid, she went quickly to the telephone in her sitting-room, and rang up Eugene Gresham's studio.

To her relief, he was there and answered the ring almost immediately.

"Are you there, 'Gene. I want to see you to-day, as soon as possible, within an hour or so. Will it be convenient for you?"

"Oh, perfectly. But," there was anxiety in his voice, "nothing is wrong, I hope."

"Oh, nothing much," she replied evasively, "only I want to talk to you—but not here."

"Why not take luncheon with me," he replied, "at half-past one and where?"

"Oh, not in any crowded restaurant," she answered a little impatiently. "At some quiet place. A tea-room—the Wistaria?"

"Very well. Then within an hour and a half."

"And, oh, Eugene," her voice detaining him, "I want the talisman. Do not fail to bring it. Do you understand?"

If Dita wore as a protecting disguise the simple and conventional dark gown which has been prescribed by certain unalterable rules of fiction as the proper costume for a lady hastening to a rendezvous, it failed of its effect, but served instead to accentuate her beauty; nor detracted in the least from her as an object of interest and comment.

And Eugene, with his fame, and his air, and his eyes, his lifted shoulder and his limp, the pointed laurel leaves seeming to gleam through his cloud of hair, handed her from her motor-car with the manner of courts, his hat in hand, to the admiration of the passers-by. The whisper ran: "Eugene Gresham and the beautiful Mrs. Hepworth." They passed through a gaping aisle. They entered the tea-room to the craning of necks. Poor souls! This was their measure of seclusion. Beauty and genius! Fame and wealth! It is a combination New York loves. She serves them up to her multitudes on a salver.

They were successful, however, in finding a remote table beneath swaying purple clusters of artificial wistaria and a dimly mellow light. And while Eugene ordered the luncheon, Dita glanced about her with a sensation of relief; new surroundings always seem to hold out the alluring if frequently vain promise of new thoughts and this was the beginning of adventure, of that new life of infinite variety she meant to live at last.

Eugene turned from the waiter, and leaning across the table narrowly observed her.

"A trifle pale," he remarked. "Mad Dita!" reproachfully and yet tenderly. "I hope all that atmospheric unpleasantness—mental, I mean, did not come boiling and seething to the surface after I left last night. I hoped the sirocco had spent itself before I left. But doubtless Hepworth understands how you are affected by a storm."

"I'm afraid I did make rather a scene," she admitted, her lashes on her cheek. "However, that is neither here nor there."

He drew a breath of relief.

"Then it is all over, the atmosphere cleared and we are to begin our sittings to-morrow." He smiled in anticipation and laughingly drew her picture upon the air.

"No," she shook her head, and spoke more reluctantly than before, "Cresswell has requested me not to have my portrait painted just now. He is kind enough," her smile was shadowy, "to think that there is no particular danger of an immediate waning of my beauty and he desires me to wait a few months."

"But that is impossible! Incredible!" he scowled with irritation and threw himself back in the chair. "Oh, what a sirocco, what a sirocco it must have been!" He shook his head back and forth and then dropped it in his hands, studying the pattern of the table-cloth as though it were the map of the situation. "To pass over my disappointment"—he lifted his head and mechanically pushed about some of the dishes the waiter placed before him on the table—"ignore it, let it go. I'm not going to press that now; but there are other things to be considered. It is known that I am to do your portrait. It was openly discussed last night. All this must be taken into account. That is for appearances as far as you are concerned. Then regarding me. I am not a paper-hanger or house painter to be engaged and then dismissed at the whim of a millionaire. I can not accept a commission from Hepworth and permit him to cancel it by a negligent message, sent through a third person. Absurd!" He frowningly bit a finger. "My plans and arrangements must be concluded for months ahead. They can not be thrown askew like this. Oh, Dita, what did you do, what did you say that brought this about? I worked like a Trojan last night to avert anything of the kind."

She did not answer, but sipped her tea with downcast eyes and he saw that the lashes on her cheeks were wet.

"Ah, Dita," his voice fell to a charming note of tenderness, a note to stir any woman's heart, with the purple and white of the wistaria clusters swaying above their heads and the mellow light reflected in his eyes, his eager eyes which pierced life's stained and sordid curtain and saw the wonder and miracle of beauty; and it was this power to discern the eternal vision which illuminated his ugly, irregular, fascinating face upon which work and dreams and experience had stamped their impress. "You can not fancy what it means to me to paint your portrait now. I've painted it before, crudely, in boyhood, and experienced then a casual delight in the effort to portray a beautiful thing, and wrest a few new secrets of art from the portrayal. That was all. But now," his voice without being raised, yet lifted exultantly, "but now—my heart is swept with insurgent seas at the thought of what it means. I am lover and artist, fused in a fire of white enthusiasm. The lover sees, divines what the artist can only guess at, and the artist offers to the lover a perfected technique. I feel the stirring of this power to catch your loveliness, Dita, and fix it on canvas imperishably. It would be the great achievement. That is in the background of every artist's thoughts. It is his pillar of cloud by day and his pillar of fire by night. The great achievement!" He dreamed over it a moment. "I would paint the South in you, Dita, 'warm and sweet and fickle is the South.' Ah! I thought I loved you then. I thought I loved you the evening we parted, but I know now that I have never really loved you before or I could not have given you up."

They were almost alone, nearly every one had left the room. A long trail of wistaria blew before her eyes. The light glowed through the silken, yellow shades. The South! She smelled roses and jasmine. It seemed to her for one bewildering moment as if her heart had indeed blossomed in purple and red. She smiled lingeringly, sweetly into his eyes.

"The portrait's only postponed, Eugene, look at it in that way." The words recalled her to herself with a start. This was paper wistaria and electric light. She was no longer a girl in a flower-scented, green old garden about to pose for a boyish and impatient artist. Here she was, in spite of all her vows to the contrary, yielding to Eugene's spell without a struggle. She was quite sure of his charm and magnetism, but what she doubted now was her own heart.

"'Ah, the little more and how much it is. And the little less, and what worlds away,'" she murmured beneath her breath, wondering unhappily if she were born to doubt everything.

"But I can't and I won't submit to a postponement." He was now both impatient and impassioned.

"It is not final," she explained. "Do take it as a postponement, nothing more. He has his reasons—oh, they are not what you suspect. He is not jealous. He is too big for that. It is something I can not go into now." Her sentences were disjointed. She seemed almost incoherent to him. "Let it be so for the present. I implore, no, I insist, that there be no explanations. But I must go, it is getting late," she started as if to rise; then sank back in her chair and held out her hand. "Oh, the amulet, Eugene."

"I haven't got it," he threw out both empty hands and looked up at her from under his brows with the expression of a naughty child. "Now listen, Dita, before you get angry, although you're so wonderful when you're angry that any one might be forgiven for tempting you into that state; but after you called me up, the Nasmyths, those English people you know, mother and daughter, were at the studio, and I was so intent on getting them away in time to meet you, the mother is the most interminable talker, that I finally bundled them out of the door and came with them, with never a thought of the amulet."

"'Gene, how like you!" Her face was full of dismay. "Cresswell especially asked me to get it to-day, and I don't think he believed for one moment that clumsy fib I told about having it mended."

"I'll go at once and get it, and bring it to the house," he said contritely. "You can make any explanation—"

"No, no more explanations," she said decisively. "They are perfect spider-webs, the most involving things any poor fly can tangle himself up in. They are, to mix metaphors, the quicksands of any situation. They make of the simplest matter a problem of complexities."

"What does that go for?" Gresham tilted his head on one side and studied her. "Does it mean that you and Hepworth quarreled about me, last night?"

73

She looked back at him in inscrutable pondering, as if considering the point, wondering, in fact, whether she and her husband really had quarreled about him.

"No explanations, Eugene, that's fixed."

"As you will," in careless assent. "But, Dita," again that ardent note of tenderness, warming his voice, and stirring her heart with all those intimations of romance which she had never known. "We might as well accept the inevitable, accept it with joy, face the light quite fearlessly. We might as well see clearly at last, what for years we should have known and believed and welcomed with all our hearts—that we belong to each other."

Her quickly lowered eyelids veiled the sudden glow of her eyes. "Perhaps," she whispered, "only I want time to think it out, to be sure of myself. I—I've grown cautious."

He looked at her with the smile that could say so many things and to her said but one. "Take time then, Dita, but permit me to pray that it will not be long. And I—I shall await with what patience I may that dazzling morning when you will open your beautiful, dreaming eyes, and know at once and for ever that you are at last awake. When you will say, 'This is my day of love, this is my hour and Eugene's! The world may go.' Take your days or months, Dita. I give them to you, for I know that every hour that passes will bring you nearer to me."

Famous artist, famous lover! Men saw his irregular, swarthy face, his lifted shoulder, his limp, and wondered. But women saw the experiences and aspirations and dreams that that face held, they saw the smiles which said so many things exquisitely, they felt the subtle, intuitive comprehension of every word, an understanding which held no condemnation, but was as warming and stimulating as sunshine. His love-making was as delightful and perfect as his art.

But again she threw off the sweet, poignantly sweet influence and strove to think clearly.

"You had your chance, Eugene, before I was married. I would have listened to you then, the night before you sailed for Europe, but you didn't believe in me, you showed it plainly." Angry tears glittered in her eyes at the remembrance.

"Ah, how could I?" His smile was at once cynical and tender. "I knew your temperament, that craving, artistic temperament. It is much like my own. We spring from the same stock, remember. You had all the inherited love of luxury and beauty as I told you then and you were starved, starved, Dita, and in a state of revolt. Your imagination was aflame with what Hepworth offered. And I—" he threw out his hands with a disclaiming gesture, "Where was I? My feet on shifting sands, I hadn't touched bedrock then. Ah, well, what's the use? The past is past. It's the future we face. My heaven, Perdita, what a future!"

His eyes held her, drew her. Involuntarily, she swayed toward him. Then, impatiently, as if resenting her own attitude, she rose to her feet.

Dita drove home, with the faint smile still lingering about her lips, still dreaming in her eyes. She drove through the park, green still in spite of frost. A mist palely irradiated by the sunshine it obscured enveloped the landscape in a sort of opaline enchantment and unsubstantiality.

It was with a sigh of regret that she entered her own house. She felt as if she had wilfully shut the door on the wooing and pensive autumn without and gone into the bleak and wintry atmosphere of regret and puzzle and doubt.

But as she moved listlessly across the hall a servant handed her a note from her husband.

She tore it open and read it. Then she read it again. It seemed to her that the rustle of the paper was like the crackle of thorns, and the fool's laughter associated with it. She had meant to manage this situation in her own way, to keep her hand well on the lever, and behold it was all arranged for her.

Very briefly the letter informed her that Hepworth's western interests would require his personal supervision for several months. That he hoped she would endeavor to make herself as comfortable and happy as possible and arrange her time in any way that best suited her. That was all. But as she walked to her own apartments it seemed to her that the air echoed and rang with the arid and mirthless laughter of fools.

CHAPTER IX

A TELEPHONE CALL

Maud Carmine was slowly pulling off her gloves before the fire in the old-fashioned drawing-room of the old-fashioned down-town house where she and her mother lived alone. It was not five o'clock, but the evenings were so short now that she hesitated whether or not to turn on the lights, but the firelight was brilliant and so much more attractive than electricity, no matter how softly shaded that might be.

Yes, the firelight was so bright that in its radiance she could see her figure reflected in the long mirror between the windows with its ornate and early Victorian frame. She walked forward and standing before it gazed at herself with a little smile. She was not a pretty woman, but she was certainly a striking and attractive one and quite beautifully gowned. That was the most noticeable thing about her, the *dernier cri* worn with style and distinction. Her heart went out in gratitude to Perdita.

While she stood there still surveying herself Wallace Martin was announced.

"And no tea here for you," said Maud. "I've been out all afternoon. Mother is gadding somewhere at this unconscionable hour, so I suppose they thought I didn't want any. I'll send for some and it will be here in a jiffy."

"I do want some, and some solid substantial bread and butter," confessed Martin. "I'm hungry. I'm dining out to-night, but the dinner is set for some unholy late hour, and I've been at a rehearsal all afternoon."

"A rehearsal of your own play?"

He nodded. "My very own," he said. "One of the million or two I've written has actually been accepted."

"Oh, Wallace!" She held out her hands, her interest and pleasure showing plainly in her voice. "I am more than delighted. It seems too good to be true."

"Don't be too enthusiastic yet," he strove to speak dryly. "It may be accepted by the managers, it is still a question whether it will be accepted by the public. It's run one gantlet, but whether it will run two remains to be seen."

"Oh, Wallace," she cried again. "How can you be so pessimistic and calm and calculating and all that? Why, I should be off my head with joy."

"I am," he said tersely. "Maud, don't tell any one, but I feel like a Wright aëroplane."

"I won't breathe it," she promised gaily, "but please don't add to the fame I'm sure you're going to get from that play, by flying over the housetops to rehearsals. Oh, here is tea, muffins, bread and butter, cake. Anything else you'll have?"

He sank back contentedly. "Nothing but to insist that you tell that 1820 butler of yours that you're not at home to any one else. It's too deliciously cosy to be spoiled by women simpering and rustling and men lounging and clattering in. Just the firelight—it's a little early for fire, but this evening is quite chilly—and the tea-kettle singing in that nice homey way, and even a big Persian cat on the hearthrug. It's 'ome and 'eaven. And what a contrast to last night! Better a dinner of herbs like this, where love is, than the stalled ox of yestere'en."

A faint blush seemed to tinge Maud's cheek, but it may have been, after all, but the flickering firelight.

"Last night wasn't awfully pleasant, was it?" she said with a little sigh.

"Pleasant! It was deadly. Poor Maud!" helping himself to more bread and butter. "How hard you worked!"

"How silly you are!" she cried indignantly. "Perfectly absurd the way you all acted. Horrid-minded creatures, bored and trying to make a situation out of nothing. Eugene Gresham and Dita have known each other for years. There is even some kind of a southern relationship between them, quite near, I believe."

"La, la!" said Wallace, again helping himself generously this time to cake, "your loyalty is beautiful, but don't let it drive you to take a stand you may have to abandon."

"Wallace!" she turned from him indignantly and the firelight showed that her eyes were full of tears.

"I mean it just the same." He placed his tea-cup on the table and bent toward her. "Look here, Maud, your friend, Mrs. Hepworth, is a very pretty woman, but she isn't a very bright one."

"That is just where you are mistaken," she returned. "She is extremely clever but you don't seem to understand how much training and environment have to do with those things. Take a woman as pretty as Dita, a woman who has been beautiful and admired from her babyhood—she has always been the center of attraction, she has never had to observe people closely, to study their moods and characteristics, never has had to try to please." There was a depth of mournful experience in Maud's tone. "Therefore she seems to carry things with a high hand, seems to lack subtlety and finesse and deference to the opinions of others. Therefore, you, seeing this, immediately put it down to lack of brains. It is a stupidity unworthy of you, at least it is a snap-shot judgment, a lack of that careful, sympathetic study and analysis of character which I should fancy would be necessary to you as a playwright."

He sat for a moment or two, with hands loosely clasped between his knees, gazing into the bed of glowing coals. This attitude and silence on his part continued for some minutes. "There!" he turned around so suddenly that she jumped, "I've given due and careful consideration to all you have to say and I will repeat my original statement. Mrs. Hepworth is a very pretty woman, but she isn't a very bright one, not bright enough to be ordinarily discreet."

Her shoulders twitched petulantly. "Wallace! The blot on your character is that you are a bit of a gossip, yes you are, and you mingle with a lot of idle people who have nothing better to do than to spend time that might be put to valuable uses in making mountains out of mole hills. Truly, it's an idiotic mental employment that is not worthy of you."

"Maud, you rouse me to argument; you do, really. I am not talking about Mrs. Hepworth's very manifestly displayed interest in Gresham last night. That might be attributed to half a dozen different causes. She might have had a row with her husband or dressmaker, or have been so bored by the happy family group gathered about her that she was ready for anything. Any one could see that she was rather out-of-sorts, excited and reckless and all that. I am not even thinking of last night, and I will immediately withdraw any aspersions I may seem to have cast on Mrs. Hepworth's brain power, if you will tell me why she gave Eugene Gresham that old trinket, amulet, talisman or whatever it is?"

Maud began to laugh, quite naturally at first, and then she stopped suddenly. She remembered the scene of the night before, the empty space in the tray. She remembered Cresswell Hepworth's surprise, and Dita's sullenness.

"But you heard Dita last night say that it was broken and that it was being mended," she protested, but some way her protestations sounded flat and unconvincing in her own ears.

"Yes, and you remember that she glanced quickly at Eugene Gresham before she answered. You also remember that Hepworth, in the innocence of his heart, explained that the old legend or tradition which had been connected with the charm for centuries had been that it could neither be bought nor sold, but that it could only be given away, given away with the heart's love of the possessor, and in that case it would prove a blessing to both him who gave and him who took."

Martin stooped and lifted the Persian cat upon his knees. "Well, my dear Maud, the end of that story is that Gresham has the amulet."

"If that is true," she flashed back, "he took it to be mended for her."

"The circumstances do not seem to point that way," he said mildly. "Really, Maud, it's the deuce of a mix-up, and I'm simply trying to prepare you for the worst. You know those English people, the Nasmyths, in draggled tweeds and velveteens; the mother wears an India shawl, and the daughter a hat which looks as if it were made of carpet. Well, they were at the Hewstons' to luncheon to-day and they had just come from Eugene Gresham's studio where they had been pottering about the best part of the morning, although Alice Wilstead said their boots and their faces looked as if they had been chasing over plowed fields. Well, they were yelping about Gresham like all other women, and raving about the beautiful things he had, and Mrs. Nasmyth told how she got to poking about on a table and found your friend's amulet; and she, of course, made an awful scream about it, and Gresham, who, she naïvely remarked, didn't seem any too pleased at her discovery, explained that it was a good-luck charm, of very ancient workmanship, which had been given to him by a dear friend, and then he gently and firmly locked it up before her eyes in a little cabinet."

"Horrid creature!" murmured Maud.

"Who?" said Wallace eagerly. "You can't possibly mean Gresham, do you, Maud? What!" his tones expressed a wondering delight as she mutely but emphatically nodded her head. "To hear a woman speak thus of that hero of romance! Never has such a grateful sound saluted my ears. Never! Maud, I am really afraid I am going to hug you."

"You are going to do nothing of the kind." She could not help laughing, although she was seriously worried.

"Well, we'll waive it for the present," he conceded, again sinking languidly back in his chair, "but that isn't the worst. I told you that it was the deuce of a mix-up, and so it is. To continue now on page eight hundred and ninety-nine, the Nasmyths babbled all this out at luncheon, and old Hewston got perfectly apoplectic. He swelled up and became purple and emitted the most dreadful snorts and whiffles, and grunts and groans, until finally just as his wife and Alice Wilstead thought he was going to fall down in a fit, he got up and puffed away from the table, and Alice and Mrs. Hewston rushed after him, leaving the poor Nasmyths to take care of themselves. And not one thing could those two women do with him. You know what an obstinate, pig-headed, meddlesome old thing he is— and his head was set on jumping into his car and off to tell Hepworth as quickly as possible and, my dear Maud, that is what he did. Alice Wilstead said that she and Mrs. Hewston hung on to his coat-tails up to the very moment he entered the car, begging, praying, beseeching, imploring. She said he dragged them all the way across the sidewalk and literally kicked himself free from them." Martin threw back his head in a great burst of laughter in which Maud very feebly joined.

"I wish I'd been there," she said regretfully. "He'd only have got in that motor over my dead body; but, Wallace, when did you hear all this?"

"I met Alice Wilstead limping up the avenue, on her way home, and she told me about it."

"I wish—" began Maud, but she was interrupted by a summons to the telephone. When she returned to the room a few moments later, her face was graver than ever.

"I'll have to leave you, Wallace," she said. "You can stay here with the cat and the fire and the tea-kettle if you want to. Perhaps mother will come in, but Dita wishes me to come to her at once."

CHAPTER X

OUT OF THE GILDED CAGE

Prompt as Maud was in responding to Dita's plea for her immediate presence, Dita was equally prompt in hurling herself upon her friend's sympathetic bosom.

Maud had been shown at once to the sitting-room of Mrs. Hepworth's personal suite of apartments, and there Dita sat in the dim and depressing gloaming of the unlighted chamber, a figure of dejection.

She had not even removed her hat, but sat brooding in the twilight until Maud's entrance roused her and she flung herself across the room and into the latter's arms with the impetuous rush of a cyclone.

Dita was temperamentally far more given to anger than to tears, but the strain of the last two days had culminated now in a burst of wild weeping, and Maud found it necessary to soothe and calm her before she could venture to inquire into the immediate cause of her friend's very poignant and unfeigned distress; so she applied herself to the task of consolation with only vague conjectures as to the cause for grief.

She was able, however, from Dita's almost incoherent statements, to patch together a fairly accurate idea of what had occurred.

"Just read this letter," Dita thrust the sheets into Maud's hand. "Oh, you can not, not in this light. Wait a moment," she touched a button and the room was flooded with a rose-colored radiance. Maud stepped nearer one of the lamps and gave her most earnest attention to the words Cresswell Hepworth had written. His utterance through the medium of the pen, was brief, self-controlled, restrained and to the point. And as Maud read his well-considered words, something like a feeling of despair swept over her.

"He has gone, actually gone," cried Dita, as Maud handed the letter back to her without comment. "Gone," she repeated the words as if the fact in itself were quite unbelievable. She crushed the letter in her hand and threw it on the floor. "He will be gone months, looking after his mines and railroads and I'm to stay here. He never even said good-by to me, and this," she touched the crumpled ball of paper contemptuously with her foot, "gives me very plainly to understand that it is a virtual separation. Oh," she jerked the pins out of her hat and sent that plumey velvet head-covering spinning across the room, then turned to her calm and sympathetic friend with a real fear and a real appeal in her eyes. "What am I going to do? For a few months it will be all right, and then people will begin to talk like everything. And you know how it will appear. Every one will say that Cresswell discovered that I was having an affair with some one, Eugene, of course, and that he, Cresswell, and I had a row and that he refused to live with me longer, but that he nevertheless was so chivalrous that he turned over this house and the country places to me. Oh, dear, why did I have to have a sirocco?"

"Heaven knows," said Maud. "Let it be a lesson to you. Never have another one. There, there, dear, I didn't mean any reproaches or I told-you-sos. So stop howling or you'll mar your beauty permanently. Oh, now, don't lift your head and glare at me indignantly and say you hope you will, that it's never been anything but a curse to you. I've been too plain all my life to listen with patience to anything of the kind. Now, let me think." She sat with finger on lip deeply considering, while Dita still punctured the silence with loud occasional sobs.

"You will have to travel," she said decisively. "Yup will have to travel until people begin to talk and then you will have to keep on traveling until they stop talking. But oh, Dita, can't you try and patch it up?"

Her words gave fresh impetus to Perdita's gradually decreasing sobs. "You do not know him," she wept, "and to tell the truth, neither do I; but I have enough of an understanding of him to know that he always considers a step very thoroughly before he takes it, looks well into the chasm before he leaps, and it's no use trying to get him to change his mind when he has decided what course he means to pursue. Anyway, I do not wish it. I want to be free, but not this way. Oh, was ever a woman placed in such a position as I? I believe Cresswell would forgive anything but the sin of not knowing one's own mind and I had to confess to him last night that I wasn't sure of mine or of my heart either. He has a contempt for me, of course, and," rising restlessly and moving about, "I can't and won't accept his contempt, and I can't and won't continue to live on his money and potter about his old houses. I feel as if I would rather die."

"But, dearest," cried Maud bewildered. "What else is there for you to do? What else can you do?"

"Nothing apparently," she said. Her dark gown fell about her in the long lines of perfect grace. As she stood there, beautiful as the tragic muse, her great eyes transfixed Maud with her scorn, but the scorn was not for her friend, but for herself. "What can I do? I am about the most useless creature on all this green earth. I sit and cry at a situation which tortures my pride, instead of coming to a decision. I made a beggarly pittance trying to earn my own living, and I won't go back to that kind of life, a disgusting, sordid, scrimpy life, which stifled every generous impulse or spontaneous action. I will not go back, I will not give up all the things I love and have become accustomed to. I was born to this. I love it, and will have it, but not on these terms.

"I haven't been utterly futile here, as I was in those other circumstances. I have made Cresswell Hepworth's upholstery, stiff houses, 'decorated and furnished by the most expensive and artistic firms,' look really livable and lovely. Truly, haven't I? Great artists have raved over them. Oh, I'm not afraid of velvets and tapestries and embroideries. I have no burgeois reverence for them. Color was always like clay to me. I always long to take it and mold it into new combinations. Why, I couldn't keep my hands off a rainbow if I got a chance at it, even the angels couldn't shoo me away." She was in one of her swift, mercurial changes of mood, her mouth dimpling, her eyes sparkling. "I'm not afraid of all the splendor of color or of all the gorgeously rich materials that God or man ever devised. I ache to take them and combine them and melt them together and contrast them. I'll dare any combination to get an effect I want, an effect that haunts me, and is like music in my consciousness. Isn't it strange that I can do anything I like with great heavy draperies? I wave my hand at them and they fall into just the lines I want. I can get all kinds of effects in a room, but give me a little palette with little gobs of paint on it, and little, little brushes and I can't do even a decent lamp mat. That is one reason Eugene and I have always understood each other so well. He, too, knows the call of color. Oh, stop looking that way, as if I were going straight to shipwreck just because I mention Eugene. The important thing to consider now is what I am going to do."

"I've told you once," said Maud, with settled conviction; "travel."

"On Cresswell's money?" bitterly. "Well, I suppose you think it's either that or huddling into some black hole and attempting to earn my living again—a phrase that's the synonym for me of a cheap and nasty experience, but there must be some way out. No, I am utterly wasted, futile, ineffective. I do not believe, I solemnly do not believe, that I have one single, solitary gift in this world except being pretty."

"Look at me!" said Maud with a rather whimsical, cynical little smile. "I think that I'm the living proof of one of your especial gifts. Why, Dita, my dear, I'm a creation of yours. I'm considered one of the most stunning women in town and about the best dressed and," Maud's really soft and attractive smile transfixed her face, "I've won, I am really beginning to dare to believe it, the interest and I hope the affection of the only man I ever cared for and who never gave me a glance when I was just 'that plain Maud Carmine, who is musical, you know.' Oh, I mean Wallace, of course," blushing. "I haven't got over the wonder of it yet, I assure you. I'm still mentally pinching myself and saying, 'If this be I.' Think of it, Dita! I know the treasures of the socially humble, if any one does. I always had position, but that amounts to very little in these days, unless one has other things to back it up. It has been gradually losing importance, pushed to the wall by money, the ability to entertain, personal charm and good clothes, an air, a flare, a wit; until now the poor, solemn, superannuated thing, so long unduly revered, is really trotted back into the corner. Yes, I had position, but not recognition. The back seats for me, so I rubbed along on my music and conversation as best I could, poor fool! And then you came, and waved your magic wand over me, took me in hand, and the world began to appraise me at your valuation."

"That was nothing," said Dita carelessly. "I just have the knack of seeing people as they ought to be. I could do what I did for you with anybody, if they would only let me. You were nice and plastic and put yourself entirely in my hands."

"Plastic!" echoed Maud. "You mean hopeless! But turn about is fair play. Take the advice I offer you, and travel. If you say the word we'll start for Japan to-morrow. And you needn't touch a penny of your husband's money either, my child. I have enough for both of us."

"Maud, you're a darling." Dita smiled in warm appreciation. "But—"

"But, Dita," Maud's voice held both fear and appeal, "if you do stay here, you will not, you must not see Eugene Gresham."

Dita smiled at her again, inscrutably. "An idea has come to me," she said, quite irrelevantly, "a dazzling idea. I really believe that it is the solution of the whole matter."

She considered this dazzling idea, her eyes growing brighter every moment.

"Oh, Maud, Maud!" she cried, clasping her hands, "what an inspiration! I'm going on my own again. Yes, I am. Don't look so horrified. I know I've grouched and fussed a lot over my past efforts in that direction, but you see I tried to do things in a small way, cotillion favors and such, and it didn't suit me. It wasn't my *métier*, not my way. I loathe detail. I can do things on a big scale or not at all. You know that. And my present idea means the big scale. When I first came to New York I regarded it as the great adventure, but then I didn't know how to go about anything. I was as ignorant as a baby of everything—everything. The tremendous professional skill required, my own ineptitude, the utter inadequacy of my poor, amateur accomplishments, my entire ignorance of business methods, all frightened, dazed, stupefied me, but now, now, I just believe I'll have another try."

89

"Oh, what *have* you got in your head now?" cried Maud in frightened resignation.

"You see it's like this," Dita ignored the question and continued to follow her own train of thought. "New York demands one of two things of the stranger who comes knocking at her gates, either training or a new idea. She can take care of any trained person, but if she has to conduct the educational process, she does it with a club. Now I'm going back to her with my new idea. Oh, I was crushed a bit ago, but now I am really enjoying myself as I have not done since the first dazzle of marrying Cresswell and seeing his money turn itself so easily into the beautiful things I had longed for all my life. But I've been getting tireder and tireder of being the twittering canary in the gilded cage. Cresswell opened the door last night and now I'm going to fly put, but in a totally different direction from the one he expects me to take." She laughed delightedly. "Oh, do you think New York will listen to my new idea?"

"She'll listen to Mrs. Cresswell Hepworth," said Maud dryly. "It won't make much difference about the idea, whether it's new or old." She thought of a conversation Hepworth's friends had held at the wedding breakfast and sighed reminiscently. "I'm afraid you're making Cress rather a background."

"Why not?" said Dita cheerfully and defiantly. "Serves him right, going away in the fashion he did and putting me in such a position. 'Moses an' Aaron,' as my old mammy used to say, you needn't try to dissuade me. You'll be as crazy about the idea as I am when I unfold it to you. The twittering canary is going to hop out of the gilded cage, and build her own nest. It's the great adventure. It is to live. Won't Cresswell open those sleepy eyes of his when he sees this move of mine on the chessboard? I'm done with failure, this venture of ours is a success before it's begun."

CHAPTER XI

A DOLL OR A BOX OF CANDY

Perdita, being one of those ardent, mercurial creatures who run with winged feet to meet every event in life, whether it be joyous or disastrous, had encountered her bad quarter of an hour the morning after the dinner party.

Hepworth's, however, was postponed for a later and more lingering occasion. We euphemistically limit these seasons of judgment to quarters of an hour in speaking of them, but they are quite independent of time, and may continue through days.

Perdita had a temperamental advantage. Hers were those swift changes of mood so disconcerting to the devils of ennui and depression; but her husband's period of reaction lasted, with but little mitigation, all the way across the continent.

A most lusty and persistent demon of doubt and self-accusation boarded his car within a few hours after the train left the station, invaded his luxurious solitude and, indifferent to a chilling reception, there remained. To Hepworth, the demon's most searing insinuation was that, instead of a masterly retreat in good order, this departure of his for the other side of the continent was a virtual renunciation of all that he cared most to win and to hold. Fool and coward, the demon whispered, to quit the game just at the moment when his presence was an imperative necessity. But, although the demon was eloquent—it is an attribute of demons—and his suggestions were like red-hot pincers, it never entered Hepworth's head to turn back. On the contrary, it was characteristic that having decided on a certain course, he was not to be swayed by the demon's most subtle and ingenious arguments. He was merely rendered supremely uncomfortable by them.

He had offered Perdita her freedom and he meant it without any reservations. She should decide on her own course, follow her own leadings according to the limits of her own folly or discretion, but free she should be, and free even from any shadowy influence that his mere presence might exert. Quixotic, scrupulously so: but then that was Hepworth's way.

The demon laughed at this obstinately maintained, unalterable decision. What chance, it sardonically suggested, had any mere average man against a rival like Eugene Gresham? Women love glamour. Perdita especially adored it blindly. Most women, certainly Perdita, would rather follow the alluring, brilliant gleam of the will-o'-the-wisp, any time, than the smoky but dependable light of the useful household lantern.

These gloomy reflections served to goad and stab like so many tormenting banderillos, but Hepworth's resolution to absent himself for a time, and thus insure Perdita a free hand, remained unalterable, in fact it hardened, became like iron.

The journey over, his spirits improved; the demon was far less persistent and only occasionally showed himself. There were a number of business matters of varying importance requiring his attention, and these very fully occupied his mind. He had made his headquarters for a time at Santa Barbara.

Then, suddenly, his busy, if rather monotonous and routine existence became diversified by a series of peculiar events which, in his most wildly imaginative moments, he would never have conjectured.

One afternoon, as he sat before an open window in the villa he had taken, looking out over a wonderful garden, all fragrance and color, at the blue channel, the mountains, the distant islands gleaming fairy-like through their golden haze, the name of Mr. James Fleming was brought to him and served very effectually to rouse him from his spiritless daydreaming, on whose confines hovered the demon.

Hepworth sat up, care vanished from his brow, the depressed droop of his mouth changed to a smile. "Fleming! Jim Fleming!" he exclaimed. "Show him in at once," to the waiting servant.

Mr. Fleming wasted no time in appearing and Hepworth pushed back his chair and rose, meeting him with a hearty hand-clasp and one of his most brilliant smiles.

This was the effect the arrival of Fleming invariably produced. One might have thought from the way men greeted him that he was some great public benefactor. Quite the opposite. Hepworth, and no doubt many others, had, through him, lost thousands of dollars, but this did not in the least affect their pleasure in his society nor tarnish their confidence in his good intentions.

Fleming was about Hepworth's age, rather tall and rather stout. He had a broad, clean-shaven face, and the mouth of an orator, large, mobile, stretching across his face in a straight line and turning up sharply at the corners. His eyes, which were blue-gray, had a most ingratiating and irresistible expression of camaraderie.

During the course of his life many unkind names had been applied to Fleming, but by women, mark you, never by men. There were quantities of good wives and mothers who regarded him very much as the devil is supposed to regard holy water. Had they not reason? At the very mention of his name they had seen a certain wild, primitive gleam light the eyes of even their most staid and house-broken men, and at the sound of his voice the most tractable and responsible husbands would seem to hear again the pipes of Pan, and forgetful of duty, daily bread and family obligations would follow eagerly whither those wild notes led.

Beyond question Fleming possessed that magnetic quality which opens all doors. He was at home in any society and where he was laughter flowed as wine. He had neither profession nor settled business, but always referred to himself as a "prospector—a prospector of the old school."

The first gay greetings over, Mr. Fleming established himself in a comfortable chair, and said without preamble, but with his usual devil-may-care nonchalance, "I've come to ask a favor of you, Cress, a mighty big favor."

Hepworth mechanically stretched his hand out toward his check book.

"Oh, it's not money I want this time," said Fleming easily. "It's no favor to me to lend me money. That's always spent on others. Anyway, I've got more than I can handle for once. You see, it's this way. I've got to go over to Idaho. I've just got wind of a big thing there, a big thing. Two boys I know want me to go over and look at it and I'm off to-day. Biggest thing that's been struck in years, they tell me. Both of them stone broke. Didn't have enough money to pay railway fare. Stole rides, practically no food for a week. If there's anything in it, I may be good enough to allow you to finance it."

"Let me see," said Hepworth reflectively, "according to the invariable law of ratio, I'm about due to win on some of these ventures of yours I've so obligingly financed."

Mr. Fleming solemnly and sadly shook his head. "Set a beggar on horseback and sooner or later he'll show his rags. The born millionaire! You show all the degenerate earmarks." He pointed the finger of scorn at Hepworth. "Even if I hadn't come along you would still have been a millionaire, climbed to it on some one else's shoulders. Entirely forgotten the old days, haven't you? Why who," explosively, "laid the foundation of your soul-deadening fortune? Me. Myself. Well, that's what a man has to expect in this world. But seriously, Cress, I do want you to do something for me."

"Don't frighten me in this way then," said Hepworth. "If it isn't money, I'm getting apprehensive. You're in some scrape and I've got to take off my coat and work like a nigger to get you out."

"Honest to God, no," said Mr. Fleming fervently. "It's just this. You see my little girl is here to spend her vacation with me—jumped across three states and got here day before yesterday, and under the circumstances it's kind of rough on her for me to go skating off this way leaving her all alone in a barracks of a hotel and in this place where she don't know a soul. Sure's I'm sitting here, Cress, I did my best not to listen to the boys," Fleming spoke earnestly. He always had the virtue of believing profoundly in himself. "It didn't seem fair to her, you know. But, oh Lord! What's the use? You know how it is when a new property swims into my ken. I get the fever so's I can't eat and I can't sleep, and it's 'my heart in the Highlands' so's I'm like to die unless I'm up and away to that little old new mine that's just been found, seeing what's to her, anyway. And you may believe it or not," in solemn asseveration, "but all the time I'm holding back and trying not to go. I've got the cramp in my feet so that I can't hobble, but the moment I yield, and take to the path again, it's gone. That's a fact. Now," the musical note of persuasion was strong in Mr. Fleming's voice, "now all I'm asking of you, Cress, is to look in on my little girl now and then and see that she has everything she wants. She's got a sort of vinegar-faced Sue with her that she calls her maid, so she's not entirely alone; but I want to be easy in my mind about her, to know that she's got some one to fall back on if anything unpleasant comes up.

"She's pretty cute, you know. About on to everything that's going. Can take the best kind of care of herself. Has had to, poor kid. Her mother died, and you know, Cress, she might just as well have had a grasshopper for a father as me. Although I've tried, she'd tell you herself, I've tried, that is, as far as the limitations of my artistic temperament would permit. But when I feel the *wanderlust* and the *weltschmerz* and all that in my blood and hear the siren voices of new properties calling, why, the fireside fetters have got to fall, the white, clinging arms have got to unloosen their grip. That's all there is to it. You know in books how the father of a motherless daughter is always father and mother and brothers and sisters and grandmother, uncles and aunts to her? Well, I haven't been all those to Fuschia. I wouldn't have known how and she wouldn't have stood for it. She's got no particular use for fireside fetters, herself. Oh," optimistically, "I guess she'll be all right here. I'm leaving her all the money she can spend. But I just want you to keep an eye on her. Kind of see that the wheels are running all right and that she's amused and don't mope. You'll like her, you know. It's a funny thing, but everybody's just crazy and always has been about that kid."

Hepworth was not proof against the appeal in his old friend's eyes, neither was he capable of shattering Fleming's simple faith that he, Hepworth, a jaded and middle-aged person, would find Fleming's daughter a delightful and interesting charge.

Fleming's mind still ran on his child. "She's about the only thing in petticoats that has any real confidence in me," he said,

96

with pride. "It's only been once or twice in my career that I've seen a look of real friendship in a woman's eyes. The first sight of me brings that wary, on-guard gleam way back in their blue or brown windows of the soul. You can't fool a woman. They've got those intuitions, you know, and they know instinctively that I'm a born missionary to the henpecked, that it's my mission in life to bring a little cheer into the lives of those poor shut-ins, the married men; scatter a little sunshine on their path.

"By the way," as if struck by a sudden thought, "you've married since I last saw you. Some slip of a girl, I'll be bound. That's what the middle-aged millionaire's sure to do. Well, hold on to your money, Cress. Don't trust to your own fascinations. And you keep an eye on my little Fuschia, won't you?"

Manfully concealing his apprehensions, Hepworth promised to do all that lay in his power to be a father to Fleming's daughter and had the consolation of seeing his old friend depart most jauntily and evidently with a weight off his mind.

But when the door had finally closed on him Hepworth let his perfunctorily smiling face relax. But it did not remain merely grave and preoccupied, for as he continued to gaze fixedly, but unseeingly, at a large paper weight before him, his eyes narrowed and his brow contracted in a frown.

He had neither the heart, time nor inclination to spend his leisure moments amusing such an utterly spoiled, untrained, undisciplined child as he was sure Fleming's daughter must be. Allowed to choose her own path from babyhood, wilful, headstrong—oh, well, what was the use of anticipating? He'd promised to look after her, and disagreeable duty as it was sure to be, he had to see it through, and that was all there was about it.

He decided to look her up the next afternoon. Take her a doll or a box of candy. Perhaps, though, she was too old for a doll. How old was she, anyway? He had forgotten to ask Jim. Probably about twelve or fifteen years. Yes, certainly, the box of candy was safer. That was always acceptable and agreeable to any of the seven ages of women.

He sighed again, and then, as if seeking distraction, he picked up the New York newspaper he was about to open when Fleming's card had been brought to him. He surveyed it languidly, his eye roving with indifference up and down the columns. Suddenly his attention was vividly arrested.

His whole gaze, even further, his whole heart hung on a paragraph stating that Eugene Gresham had just sailed on the *Mauritania*. It was known among Mr. Gresham's friends that he had recently received a commission to paint the portrait of a princess of the royal house of Austria and that upon completing this he would go to England to finish a portrait, already begun, on a previous occasion, of the beautiful Lady Heppelwynd. Mr. Gresham, when seen on board ship a moment before sailing, would neither confirm nor deny these rumors.

The frown disappeared from Hepworth's face. What commendable discretion! Whether the credit were due Dita or Gresham mattered little. It was the admirable restraint, this delicate and unexpected regard for appearances, which Hepworth applauded. To do him justice, that was his first thought, the sober second one was profound relief that the fascinating will-o'-the-wisp was as far away from the impulsive and curious Dita as was the smoky lantern. He put the paper down and rose to his feet. Fleming's little girl should have a box of candy that was a box of candy.

CHAPTER XII

FUSCHIA FLEMING

Procrastination was a thief that had never succeeded in wresting much time from Hepworth. He was one of those rare and exemplary natures who never put off until to-morrow what they can do to-day. Never did he stand shivering on the edge of his cold bath, but plunged in immediately without pause for consideration. Obnoxious virtues these—prejudicial to any popularity among his fellow-beings, therefore it speaks volumes for him that he was able to overlive them.

This all goes to show that although the duty of keeping an eye on Fleming's daughter became more repugnant to him the longer it remained in contemplation, he yet lost no time in looking her up, as he expressed it to himself. Neither did he waver in his promise to himself fitly to celebrate Eugene Gresham's departure for other shores, but kept his vow by selecting the most gaudily decorated and wastefully beribboned box of sweets he could secure, and armed with it, as a hostage to impertinent childhood, took himself to the big hotel where Miss Fuschia Fleming was stopping.

He sent up his name to her and was very shortly informed that Miss Fleming was in the garden and would be delighted to have him join her there.

Hepworth curled his lip. What grown-up airs! Naturally, she had lost no time in turning up her hair and having her gowns lengthened since her father's departure, and he, Hepworth, would have to play up to this phase of missishness.

He was dazzled for the moment by the bright sunshine, the brilliant flowers, and mechanically followed the page, threading his way through various groups of people. Before a

99

table among the roses sat a young woman reading. The page stopped; Hepworth stopped; the young woman cast aside her book and rose.

Before a table sat a young woman reading.

"How do you do, Mr. Hepworth?" She stretched out her hand with a boyish gesture, smiling into his eyes, and the sunshine grew dim. "Won't you sit down? I've just ordered some tea. If you don't drink it, won't you tell the man to bring you something else when he comes? Father said—"

"But father is surely not Fleming, Jim Fleming," he said, firmly determined to get this absurd mistake straightened out at once.

"But father just is," she asserted as firmly. "And since you asked for Miss Fleming, I am she, Fuschia Fleming. That is my ridiculous name."

But Hepworth had so far lost his mental equilibrium that he could not immediately recover himself.

"Fuschia Fleming is a little girl," he insisted, although this time not half so positively, "and great Heavens," with one of his quick smiles, "I've brought you a box of candy and just barely escaped buying you a doll."

"I wish you had," she said. "I love dolls, especially the kind that you would bring me." There was undeniably something heady about Fuschia Fleming's glance. "And as for sweets, they're grateful and comforting to any age. You'd better give me that box at once, and I'll give you a practical demonstration of my appreciation."

Fuschia had the curliest mouth. There is no other way to describe it. It was all in ripples, not small, but looking smaller than it really was because it turned up quite sharply at the corners, like her father's. And the lashes that lay on her pale, smooth cheeks were the curliest and longest Hepworth had ever seen. Her eyes were blue, blue as the sea, and very cool and gay and inclusive. Without being sharp or speculative or inquisitive, they yet took in all the details of whatever they rested upon.

But Hepworth was a keen observer, and he noticed at once that although her pale face was for the most part alive with laughter, there was yet a certain worn look about it, as if she had been recently over-taxed and fatigued. There were faint but undeniable lines about the mouth and eyes that time had never etched there; and that blythe assured bearing, her detached, yet ready manner, were not suggestive of the ease of confident youth. They bespoke training.

Hepworth's eyes, their droop rather more pronounced than usual, were fastened on an adjacent palm, as if he demanded from it the answer to this riddle. Getting no response there, he turned his speculating eye on a tree of magnificent crimson roses as if hoping for some enlightenment from that quarter.

"Why do you not tell me all about it?" urged Fuschia gently. "What's the use of trying to puzzle me out unaided? Father has evidently told you a lot of conflicting things. I really can throw more light on the subject than any one else."

Her voice was beautiful, soft and full and creamy, with all exquisite modulations and inflections, and its music cleared Hepworth's befogged brain. He released the palm and the rose tree from the third degree to which he had been subjecting them, and leaned back in his chair as if he relaxed his mind as well as his body, smiling back at her, as confident now, and as assured as herself.

"I don't have to," he said. "I know. It's just come to me. You see your father didn't happen to mention that you are studying for the stage."

"Studying for the stage!" she cried, as if to refute him, considered, and then nodded emphatically. "Of course I am, and expect to be until I die; but hardly in the sense you mean. My field of study at the present time includes a good deal of practical experience. I've been on the stage now for three years, ever since I left school."

"On the stage!" he exclaimed. "But my dear child, under what name?"

"My own," she answered. "Oh, do not look so puzzled. It is the most unlikely thing in the world that you should ever have heard of me. I'm far from a star, just one of the humble members of first this and then that western stock company. You see, my idea was to get my training and experience before I burst upon New York. But New York is beginning to seem too iridescent a dream ever to be realized."

There was a fall in her voice, a touch of wistfulness, which Hepworth found rather touching because its pathos was both uncalculated and unconscious.

"Why?" he asked in surprise. This note of resignation in her tones, of acceptance of a disappointing, inevitable circumstance, struck him as singularly out of character and aroused his curiosity.

"It's been the same thing several times in succession now," said Fuschia, a touch of superstitious gravity in her expression. "Just as father is preparing to stake me, and I'm getting a company together to take New York by storm as Rosalind, why, father loses his last dime on a dead-sure thing. There's a law about it. The biggest winning proposition in years, always comes along just as I am ready to cross the Alps and storm Italy. Uncanny, isn't it?"

"What nonsense!" Hepworth clipped off the end of a cigar as if it were Fleming's head. "Do not let yourself be affected by such an absurdity. The only law, and I admit it's a strong and binding one, is Jim's selfishness and irresponsibility. Now my dear child," Hepworth was beginning to fancy himself enormously in the rôle of paternal adviser, "you make him give you as much as possible."

"I do," she interrupted softly.

"And you lay it all aside, very securely, never touching a penny of it—"

"What about my clothes?" another interruption.

"Never touching a penny of it," went on Hepworth firmly, ignoring these asides on her part, "until you have saved enough to finance yourself. Isn't that reasonable?"

"Ye-s," admitted Fuschia. "It is a very reasonable and sensible suggestion, Mr. Hepworth, that is," thoughtfully, "if you leave out father and me. But just get it into your head that at the moment I'd save a nice little heap, father would be hit with an overwhelming impulse to back the wrong horse, and, here's something awfully queer psychologically, Mr. Hepworth, I'd know as sure as I'm Fuschia Fleming that it was the wrong horse, and yet, I'd get inoculated with the mental virus before I'd know it, and beg him to let me in on it. And you know that father is incapable of staking half or even two thirds of his little all against any proposition he believes in. The only thing that can satisfy him and make his blood tingle is to stake the whole. No limit but the blue canopy of heaven. Limits do fret father."

Mr. Hepworth slightly lifted his shoulders. Then he dropped another lump of sugar into a cup of hot tea she had given him.

105

"I wish to seem neither irrelevant nor impertinent," he said at last, "but can you act?"

Miss Fuschia Fleming threw up her white chin and laughter bubbled unquenchable from her throat, not vain-glorious mirth, as if the fact of her superlative achievement mocked his crude question, but the unrestrained laughter of genuine amusement.

"The idea of asking an actress such a question," she said at last, touching each eye lightly and deftly with a delicate handkerchief. "You may thank your lucky stars that I don't nearly drown you with picturesque and highly colored tales of my triumphs and then hurl the full scrap-book at you. My, but you are a rash man! To ask a professional if she can act!" Again her full-throated laughter rang out delightfully and so heartily that it shook the petals from the cluster of pale golden roses she wore on her breast.

"But look here, seriously now," her laughter died quickly away, her face assumed a gravity he had not dreamed her mobile features could express, her gaze fastened upon him with a sort of hungry, passionate eagerness.

"That was a horrible question of yours," she shivered, as if the breeze blowing over the gardens from the Elysian sea chilled her. "One should know intuitively, instinctively whether an actress can act or not. Good Lord!" she brought her hand down on the table. "If you don't feel it, know it, beyond all argument, why it isn't there, that's all.

"Unless I set you dreaming, unless I suggest in this or that varying pose or expression, the whole world of women, I'm not a born actress. Training, study can make a good mechanical nightingale of me, a clever imitation of the real thing. That's all. But unless I have the chameleon quality of

106

reflecting my part, the unerring understanding of any type of woman I may be called upon to represent, how can I be an actress? What does it profit me to give the public a carefully studied, intellectual representation of Portia or Nora, or Juliet or Candida, wide apart as the poles as they may be? I must not only apprehend them, I must be them in every fibre of my being, in every cell of my brain, in every beat of my heart, or I'm nothing. Unless I can convince you that Camille and I are one in emotion and view of life, and then obliterate that impression when I speak to you as Rosalind, why I'm not an actress, not the kind I care to be, anyway."

"By Jove, my dear," cried Hepworth, "you need have no doubts on that score." He had not felt the thrill of such genuine enthusiasm for many a long day.

He forgot the delicate and uncertain state of his marital affairs, forgot the censorious world, his ennui and doubt and regret.

"I have a conviction," he said, "that Jim is going to win a lot on this new proposition of his. If he doesn't, it's all the same anyway. Why should you waste your youth and your genius in twentieth rate stock companies?"

In spite of these cheering words, her head continued to droop. Her face had grown paler, and sad were the eyes she lifted to his.

"But you asked me if I could act. You weren't sure. You didn't see me as Camille or Rosalind. You just saw Fuschia Fleming all the time."

"Of course I did." His smile was most comfortingly reassuring. "But I saw Fuschia Fleming as Juliet and Portia and all the others. I merely asked you if you could act to see what you would say. No, no, my dear, your future is written so plainly

107

that he who runs may read. No more one-night stands in dreary little towns, Miss Fuschia Fleming, but long engagements, crowded houses, enormous box-office receipts, wildly enthusiastic audiences. Can't you hear and see them? New York, London, Paris for you!"

"Oh-h!" Fuschia was herself again. She exhaled rapture in an ecstatic sigh. She rose. It is impossible to sit in moments of such high exultation. She positively seemed to soar, to tread on clouds. It was growing late and chill. Almost every one had left the garden, only a few absorbed groups remained. Fuschia was an actress. Self-expression was a necessity to her. She rested her hand, a snowflake, gratefully on his arm, she floated against him, a thistledown, and before he knew it had lightly, enthusiastically, unconcernedly kissed him on the cheek.

"You dear," she cried, "I'll repay you by showing you what I can do. To tread the forest of Arden in New York! Oh-h! But you are not going. No, no, no!"

That was what Hepworth, rather overcome by the unconventional and unexpected expression of her thanks, was preparing to do. He thought it best, but his decision was not adamantine, far from it. He always prided himself upon the open mind, and an ability to see all sides of a question, so when Fuschia suggested that he return later and dine with her, it struck him as a possible, even admirable solution of his daily puzzle how to put in the evening and he accepted without more debate, with an alacrity, in fact, bordering on gratitude.

He was therefore on time to the minute and Miss Fleming was equally punctual.

As they sat through a dinner, not elaborate, but as prolonged as if it were composed of all the courses on the menu, Hepworth was struck by the positive quality of Fuschia's beauty. It was not always so, evidently. She was as changeful as the chameleon she had spoken of. In the garden that afternoon, in her white serge frock, she had at first impressed him as a pale, rather attractive looking young woman whose charm was greater than her prettiness; but viewed in the rose-colored lights, and across the pink blossoms on their small table, she was a very wonderful creature. She was, in truth, wild with joy and her expression of it was delightful. Her eyes were blue as the sea when the sun is one vast sparkle over it, her mouth, made for laughter, grew curlier every moment. Her white evening gown was a dream.

In addition to her admirable outward appearance, Miss Fuschia Fleming was a comédienne of unsurpassed gifts. She was also witty, well-read and sweet-natured, and when she chose to exert herself she could make sixty minutes seem sixty seconds by any one's watch, even that of the grimmest old curmudgeon, and Hepworth certainly was not the grimmest old curmudgeon. He was only a very lonely and sad-hearted man whose days had been hanging heavily on his hands.

"Good old Jim," he soliloquized as he took his way homeward that evening. "He believed sufficiently in my friendship to come right to me when he was in a hole. Made no bones about it. Asked me to keep an eye on his daughter, sure enough of my affection for him to know I'd do it. I shouldn't wonder if this Idaho proposition is a good thing if it's properly financed. Jim's judgment is pretty sound. Well, we'll see, we'll see."

CHAPTER XIII

SHOCKING THE HEWSTONS

As the winter wore on the weather in New York offered daily a more violent and odious comparison to the blue seas and balmy airs of California. The cold, sullen skies, dull, damp days and piercing winds set more than one dreaming of sunshine and summer, and among the many was Alice Wilstead.

She was pondering thus, looking about her with surprise, one especially snowy, dreary winter afternoon as she took her way to Mrs. Hewston's. It was one of those thoroughly depressing days when nothing could really raise one's spirits but the inspiring glow of firelight. Mrs. Wilstead certainly looked as if she needed that and all positively cheering if not inebriating things as she entered Mrs. Hewston's drawing-room. Her piquant dark face was meant for smiles and gaiety, all of her features apparently designed to that end, for the corners of her mouth, the tip of her nose, the slant of her eyes, all inclined upward. It is a tragedy when a person of such countenance is in an introspective or melancholy mood. Sober meditations have an aging and blighting effect on the features of those born to look out upon the world with an arch and piquant interest.

Isabel Hewston roused herself a little reluctantly. She was sitting alone most comfortably in a delightfully easy chair, she had on a becoming and loose Paris tea-gown. She had resolutely put behind her the haunting specter of increasing flesh, had taken an afternoon off from the persistent and continued battle she had been forced to wage with it, and now lay, a box of sweets on the table beside her, a new novel in her hand, enjoying to the full her temporary respite. It is to her credit that she put aside her book at the most nerve-tingling paragraph without a sigh.

"Dear Alice," she exclaimed, lifting herself on one elbow, "you have a bad-news look all over you, the very rustle of your skirt proclaims it. What can be the matter?"

"Give me some tea," said Mrs. Wilstead gloomily, "and let me sit down and rest." She slowly removed her furs. "My dear Isabel, do you mean to say you do not know?"

"Know what?" asked Mrs. Hewston in bewilderment, ringing and mechanically ordering tea. "How could I possibly know anything after just getting off the steamer this morning? What has happened? You haven't been speculating, Alice, and losing all your money?"

Mrs. Wilstead hastily disclaimed any such unforgivable crime and inconsolable grief as losing money. "Then really you have not heard," she exclaimed. "Isabel, I am more worried than I can say. Lemon, please. It is stupid of you, Isabel, never to get into your head the fact that I couldn't be guilty of taking cream. To think of such a thing occurring! I had hoped that with Eugene Gresham out of the way, having the decency to go to England and France, and the papers full of his spectacular stunts, that all talk would cease and that when Cresswell Hepworth came back from that western trip that everything would be all right."

"What are you talking about?" asked Isabel Hewston with the calmness of despair. "If it isn't too much trouble, would you mind making a few explanations? Just one might suffice."

"It is that absurd, undisciplined Perdita Hepworth. She has had her head completely turned by the success of Maud Carmine and now she and Maud have gone into business together."

"Into business?" Mrs. Hewston made a tremendous clatter among the tea-cups. "Business! What can you mean? Cresswell has not failed?"

"Good heavens, no! But that is the reason he has been so long in the West. At least that is what every one says. Dita and Maud informed him of this scheme, and he, of course, expressed his opinion of the whole matter, refused to countenance it; but he couldn't do anything with such a headstrong creature as Dita, and so he simply cleared out; went West and has stayed there, while those two girls have gone stubbornly on and carried out their plans."

"Business!" Isabel still rolled her eyes in dazed speculation. "But what kind of business? What could they possibly do? Lamp-shades, menu-cards? I'm sure I've always heard that Perdita didn't make such a brilliant success when she tried that sort of thing before!"

"Menu-cards! Lamp-shades!" Alice laughed scornfully. "That's mere paper dolls to this venture. This is a business of their own invention, although Dita does take orders for house decoration also; but the main purpose is dressing the wealthy, telling the plain little daughters of the rich what to wear."

"For pity's sake!" gasped Isabel. "What sort of place is it, beauty parlors or dressmaking?"

"Oh, dear me, neither! Nothing so commonplace. They have taken a house just on the Avenue (they say it is a dream within), and you have to write for an appointment, and then if they will consider you at all they write back and set a time, and you go exactly as if you were calling, you know, and you are received by either Maud or Dita or both. Then you come again whenever they tell you, and all the time Dita is studying you just as a portrait painter would. Finally, when she feels that she has you thoroughly in mind, and is quite decided about the way you shall be clothed, she has designs made for you of hats and gowns, little water colors, you know, and sends you to her dressmaker. She also has your maid come and dress your hair before her, according to her directions. And it costs you!" Alice Wilstead pursed her mouth and lifted her brows, "It costs you! Oh, like the dickens!"

"Who is that?" said Mrs. Hewston turning.

"Only me," Wallace Martin replied modestly and ungrammatically, entering, as usual, unannounced, a privileged friend of the family, and greeting the two women with his usual barking cheerfulness.

"I just walked up home with that pretty little Lolita Withers, and, as you were only a block or two farther, I came on here."

The two women gazed at each other with a long, wondering stare. "Lolita Withers!" they exclaimed simultaneously. "Pretty!" Nothing could have been more eloquent than their tones.

"My dear Wallace," said Mrs. Hewston, finding her voice, "is this some new joke? Are you quite sane?"

"He means it for a joke," said Mrs. Wilstead, who had been peering at him curiously. "He is going in for eccentricity, or else the success of his play has gone to his head."

"Not a bit of it," replied Martin with unmoved smiles. "Lolita Withers is at present an obviously pretty girl. Any one would so consider her."

"Obviously pretty." Mrs. Wilstead had found her tongue by this time, and acrid and scoffing it proved. "That skinny, ineffective little Lolita Withers! Dull-eyed, anæmic, with stooping shoulders and wispy light hair."

"She looks like a dream of spring," said Wallace, helping himself lavishly to tea and cakes. "A sort of an evanescent beauty. Truly, yes," he affirmed, "she's been to Maud Carmine and Perdita Hepworth." He gave a great burst of laughter.

"If they can make any one believe that Lolita Withers is pretty," said Mrs. Hewston dazedly, "they are indeed benefactors of the race."

"Perdita Hepworth is a genius, a wizard. I always said so." Alice announced this with a sort of triumphant conviction. "She could make Aaron's rod blossom like the rose."

"But where did they get the money?" Mrs. Hewston's mind turned always to practical things. "If Dita really quarreled with Cress, would he—?"

"Maud's money." Martin spoke with the assurance of one possessing authoritative knowledge. "Cresswell Hepworth! Oh, no, he went off in a terrible huff because the girls laid their plans before him and told him what they were going to do. At least," he amended, "that is the idea I got from the little that Maud has occasionally told me. Yes, it's Maud's money; but they'll lose nothing, plucky girls! Double and treble it, more likely. They've already had an overwhelming success."

"I'm going to them," cried Isabel Hewston excitedly. "If they are so wonderful they ought to be able to make me look slender without my having to go to all the bother of being really slender."

"You'll have to stand in line then; that old Mrs. Peter Huff is jumping for joy and calling down blessings on their heads because they've literally transformed her three ugly daughters. Maud said they were splendid material, and Dita did wonders with them. The old lady hopes to get them married off now."

"Alice! When can we go to them?" Mrs. Hewston's voice was trembling with excitement.

"I can't go now." There was a distinct fall of disappointment in Alice Wilstead's voice. "The truth is, I'm going to California with the Warrens the first of next week. Why, what is that?"

There was a sound of some one wheezing, puffing, muttering without the door, and then the curtain was violently jerked aside and Mr. Hewston entered. His hair stood up white and ruffled about his head, his face was of a much livelier crimson than usual, and he was puffing out his lips as if blowing fire and smoke from his mouth. In one hand he was tightly clasping a newspaper.

"Willoughby! My dear!" his wife rose in consternation. "What is it, what has happened?"

For answer Mr. Hewston spread open the paper and struck it with his hand. "Read that," he cried tragically, "read that! My poor friend, driven from his home by the vagaries of a mad, irresponsible girl, his life ruined by the foolish, frivolous creature he married! Turned from his home, he was driven to this."

Wallace had seized the paper, and the two women hung over his shoulder to scan the sheet before them.

What met their eyes were huge, black head-lines above and below the pictures of Cresswell Hepworth and a very pretty woman.

The head-lines announced that the two had been in an accident in Mr. Hepworth's motor-car at Santa Barbara. Both were thrown out, but neither sustained any serious injuries. The article went on to say that Mr. Hepworth had, during his stay in the West, evinced great interest in the career of this beautiful and gifted young woman, an actress of reputation in her part of the world, but unknown in the East. It was understood, however, that she was to play a New York engagement during the coming spring, making her first bow to a metropolitan audience as Rosalind in a superb stage presentation of *As You Like It*. There was no question of the beauty of the mounting of this famous comedy, nor the strength of the company with which the young star would be surrounded, as the capital behind her was practically unlimited.

CHAPTER XIV

PUBLICITY

When the beautiful, young wife of a multi-millionaire takes advantage of her husband's absence on a prolonged and unavoidable business trip to embark upon a rather bizarre and eccentric venture of her own, it is to be expected the situation will be hugely discussed, especially in its three-fold phases—the lady first, the exact relations existing between husband and wife next, and third, the business itself.

Perhaps in this case the business should be put first, above the lady, and above any sentimental interest in marital misunderstandings, for Perdita's skill in "bedecking and bedraping" was well known among her sisters, whose ideals in bedecking were those of Paris, and who had no Greek longings to be "noble and nude and antique." And had they not for the past two years enviously regarded Maud Carmine—who had been as a walking *mannequin* among them, the living, breathing advertisement of Perdita's abilities.

Therefore from the very first business bade fair to engulf the new firm and sweep the two partners off their feet, and if the list of those who daily assembled in "Hepworth and Carmine's" reception-rooms were to be published, it would look like a social registry or a page from *Who's Who*; that is, a page with all of the masculine names carefully culled.

There were elderly ladies and young girls, and ladies in all the waning stages between the two. The elderly and waning ones all hoped before Mrs. Hepworth got through with them to look like the young girls, and the young girls, with all the enthusiasm of youth, hoped to look like Perdita Hepworth.

There arrived then, one morning, at this palace of hope, Mrs. Willoughby Hewston, who, as she stepped from her motor, glanced nervously right and left and ascended the steps of the house Perdita and Maud had taken just off the Avenue with an agility of which her best friends would not have considered her capable. This nervousness, this hurry was due to the fact that only the day before she had mentioned her intention to her husband, with the result that she was thunderously ordered not to go near the place, under penalty of his worse than censure. He gave her to understand that this would be something too terrible for her imagination even to apprehend. Consequently, Mrs. Hewston wasted no time in getting to Hepworth and Carmine's as early as possible the next morning. She would have been less than woman had she not done so.

The reception-room was spacious, sunny and restful, depending for its effect upon beautiful woods and long, unbroken lines; for color, there was the hint of ivory and tea-green, ineffably serene, and there Mrs. Hewston awaited Dita, her agitation subsiding somewhat under the calm influence of the place.

But when Dita appeared it returned in full force. "Oh, my dear," she exclaimed, "what a charming spot this is! How original! How daring of you and Maud! Oh, my dear, if Willoughby knew I was here!" She raised her hands with a gesture full of meaning. "You know that he is in such a state anyway over those newspaper articles."

"What newspaper articles?" asked Perdita. "Do you mean those that have appeared about all this?" she waved her hand comprehensively about her.

"Haven't you seen them?" Mrs. Hewston looked frightened. "Oh, my dear child, how very stupid of me. Why, why did I mention them? I supposed, of course, that you knew. But if you do not, please do not ask me anything more, for I never, never will be the bearer of bad news."

Dita stared at her in puzzled amazement for a moment and then she took her firmly by the shoulders. "Look here, Mrs. Hewston, you are frightening me dreadfully. I haven't an idea what you are talking about. Now you must tell me, indeed you must. Do you not see the state of mind in which you leave me unless you do?"

"Oh, my dear," Mrs. Hewston shook her handkerchief out of her bag, evidently preparing for its possible use. "I didn't mean to frighten you, and you shouldn't allow yourself to be so easily upset. Now, understand, no one was hurt, but those dreadful papers yesterday were full of a motor accident which occurred in California."

"Cresswell's car?" interrupted Dita quickly. "Was he—" She was about to say "injured," but Mrs. Hewston took the word from her mouth, or rather, substituted another for it.

"Alone? No, dear," shaking her head a little as at the regrettable, but to be expected frailties of men. "He was not alone. He was driving the car, it seems, with a beautiful young actress by his side. She must be a very—er—persuasive person, too, because the papers said that she is to appear here this spring in some superb production or other, and they strongly insinuated that Cress' money is behind the whole thing. But you see, that, as I said, there's nothing in it all, nothing really to worry over."

"I see," said Dita, but slowly and without enthusiasm.

"And now, my dear," Mrs. Hewston had suddenly grown quite brisk, "let's forget all this and talk of something that is more interesting to you, because it's in your line. Perdita," in her

119

most wheedling and cooing tones, "I want you to make me lovely."

"You are lovely, Mrs. Hewston."

"Oh, in a middle-aged, broad, pink kind of way, but I want you to make me look slender and lissome and girlish without all this awful dieting and exercise and these dreadfully tight corsets that make one feel as if one were nothing more nor less than blanc-mange in a tin mold. And you know you do come out of them with your flesh all fluted, just like the blanc-mange when it's set."

"You shall be quite lissome, I promise you that," said Dita consolingly, if rather absently. "Come to me again early next week and I shall have some designs for you to consider, beautiful, long folds and all that. But I can't perform miracles, you know, and you'll have to diet a little and exercise; yes, and wear the boned corset; you don't want to look like a—"

"Do not say it!" cried Mrs. Hewston nervously. "I am sure you are going to say either 'whale' or 'tub,' and I can't stand it. That's what those awful corsettières always say when I protest the least bit against their tortures.

"And Perdita, one thing more—my chin. I always say the chin is the greatest give-away a woman's got. She can get around anything else, but, no matter what she does, that chin sticks out like a cliff and reveals every year she's lived. Of course, you may try to draw off attention with a diamond dog collar or jeweled black velvets, but at the best they're only poor, miserable makeshifts; and one must wear evening dress no matter whether one has rolls of flesh or a gridiron of bones. If you don't, people either think you come from the woods or have something worse than bones or superfluous flesh to conceal. Just look at Willoughby!" Mrs. Hewston's emotions

120

overcame her here and she dabbed her eyes carefully with her handkerchief. "He is fat as a pig. He shuffles and hobbles about with the gout. He eats anything he pleases, and never thinks of cultivating a pleasant expression. Yet if I should die, he could marry again without difficulty. Oh, it's a hard world for us women! But really, I must go, dear. Just look out and see if you see Willoughby by chance, either up or down the street."

As soon as she was assured of safety and had departed, Perdita, who, fortunately for herself and her customers, had no other appointments for the morning, sent for the papers of the day before and carefully considered the incident of Mr. Hepworth, Miss Fuschia Fleming and the motor-car as set forth in the various journals.

"And so," said Perdita to herself with glooming eyes, when she had finished an exhausting perusal, "he is going to back this deserving young adventuress, who has, no doubt, played upon his sympathies, in a great spectacular presentation this spring, and in New York. Well, there will be something else spectacular. I will make this venture of ours a stupendous success now or I will know the reason why. Where on earth is Maud? She is never about when I really need her."

She frowned a moment over Maud's delinquency and then happened to remember that Miss Carmine had expressed an intention of being present at a rehearsal of one of Wallace Martin's plays. Dita then decided on the moment to drive to the theater and consult with her partner at once on the new and spectacular policy of their house which she was mentally outlining.

But first, before starting, she thoughtfully selected some of a number of photographs of herself and also of Maud. "I suppose I shall have a dreadful time persuading her," she reflected as she drove through the streets. "She has bred in the bone those old-fashioned ideals of New York when it lived in Bleecker and Houston Streets."

But curiously enough, while events of one character had led Perdita strongly to consider the adoption of a certain line of action, circumstances of a widely differing nature had impelled Maud practically to the same conclusion. Which only goes to show how clever a weaver is Fate and how wonderfully she contrasts and combines all her various threads.

For two or three hours Maud had been sitting in a dimly-lighted, empty playhouse, watching the rather dreary and disillusionizing progress of Martin's latest play.

It was an odd thing, she mournfully reflected, that Wallace never got himself, his own, bubbling, merry, joyous self, full of quirks and quips, into his plays. They would seem to have been written by a secondary personality, for they were all, without exception, intensely serious and depressing, dealing with problems of the most complex and dun-colored character.

Maud was extremely practical. She never dreamed of buoying up her spirits with any ambrosial reflections that this latest offering was "a distinct contribution to the more serious drama." Neither did she attempt to convince herself that there were enough high-browed folk in the town to keep the play on for, peradventure, three nights. No, she simply, and with her usual common sense, reserved judgment until the third act, and then after a moment of wonder that Wallace had found a firm of managers willing to undertake the production, with all the expense entailed, when they had just one chance in a million to win (in her opinion, at least), she turned to more practical issues.

"Dita and I," she remarked mentally, "have got to make a stupendous success if I want to marry Wallace, which I do, and he is going to continue to write plays, which he is. But I'll have a frightful time persuading Dita to run her business along the lines of twentieth century advertising. She has all sorts of ante-bellum ideas about stately procedure and measured methods, derived, of course, from those generations of lazy southern aristocrats."

While she mused, amid the terrific racket of moving things about the stage in preparation for the fourth act, she felt a light touch upon her shoulder, and looked up to see Perdita, pale but determined, standing beside her.

"I'll just slip into this seat beside you," said Mrs. Hepworth, suiting the action to the word. "I want to talk to you a few minutes. Now, Maudie, I know that you will not like it, but we've been doing awfully well lately, and I think it would be a good idea to put what we've made in advertisement. Of course, there's a lot we can get without paying for it. The Sunday newspapers will print pages about us, especially—especially if we let them have some of our most stunning pictures and allow those interviews where the artists sit and make sketches of you."

Maud looked at her business partner as one who, bidden to rub a magic ring on his finger and wish, sees his wish come true. Here was Perdita approaching her tactfully, and timidly entreating her to do the very thing that was in her mind to accomplish. She could not grasp it, but sat staring at her companion in an amazement so profound that it bereft her of speech.

Perdita misinterpreted the silence. "I've got to make a red-and-yellow success," she exclaimed with emotion. "I've—I've just got to be in the newspapers. Don't take it in this cold, reproving way."

"My dear Perdita," Maud spoke with crisp distinctness. "I'm not! It's your attitude of mind, not your sentiments, that surprises me. The latter are my own. You," she continued virtuously, "are probably actuated by your vanity; I, by my heart. Look at that!" she waved one hand toward the stage, "or rather don't look at it. Now let us come to an understanding. You know that I have always loved Wallace. You know that he has lately loved me. You also know what it costs me a year to be one of the best-dressed women in New York and maintain my newly acquired reputation for good looks; consequently the business has to make handsome returns. We live in the twentieth century under artificial conditions, and it's no use pretending it's Arcadia and the simple life. It's not. We're hothouse blossoms, Perdita, products of this great forcing bed, New York, and we might just as well adapt ourselves to conservatory conditions. Wallace wouldn't look at me if I were a hardy annual. He didn't when I was what God and nature made me. But Wallace suits me, child though he is, in many ways, and I can do a great deal with him. I may even," but Maud's tone had lost its high confidence and was a trifle dubious now, "I may even make a playwright of him."

"Why, here he is now with—with Eugene Gresham," interrupted Perdita. This was but the second time Perdita had seen Eugene since his return a few days before.

Out from the wings stepped the two men and then clambered over the footlights and the orchestra space, and hastened down the aisle to join Mrs. Hepworth and Miss Carmine, who had now a number of large photographs spread over their knees, intently studying them.

"Good morning," Wallace shook hands exuberantly with both women. "Went splendidly, didn't it? We're going to have the first act over again."

"Very impressive, very," said Gresham, who looked in the best of health and spirits.

Maud cast one withering look at him, but it glanced lightly off, turned aside by his smile. He saw it, however, and as quickly as possible got into a seat on the other side of Perdita.

"Have you seen the papers?" he asked happily. "Blessings on Miss Fuschia Fleming. I shall do my humble best to keep the ball rolling. As soon as she appears in New York, I'm going to put in a request to do her portrait. Something bizarre, weird and splotchily thrilling, you know. Quite violent. That will keep a crowd around it from dawn to dark as soon as it's exhibited. It doesn't make the least difference whether she has any ability or not. She may be, and probably is, the most awkward, scrawny and nasal of western actresses; what of it? With Hepworth for her angel and Gresham for her painter, her vogue is secure. And Perdita, Rosita, your freedom is that much nearer."

"Eugene," Perdita's eyes flashed, "I think it extremely bad taste, even vulgar, of you to talk in that vein."

And Eugene hastened to retrieve his blunder, and soon Perdita, who was never long impervious to his spell, was smiling once more.

Miss Carmine, however, was of sterner stuff. She did not wince, although she saw that there was no remedy for Wallace's malady but the knife, and he, unwittingly, wasted no time in precipitating his destiny.

"What are you doing with all those photographs of yourself and Mrs. Hepworth?" he asked.

"We are going to give them to some reporters, who are getting up stories for the Sunday papers."

"Maud!" Martin spoke in the deep, pained tones of his leading man. "Maud, I have said nothing. In fact I admired and approved when you and Mrs. Hepworth went into this business venture. But such methods for you, for her! Do you not feel that you owe something to yourselves, and that she at least owes something to Hepworth? Oh, of what are you thinking?"

"Money," said Maud succinctly. "Something you evidently are not thinking of." She glanced toward the stage.

"I hope not," he answered stiffly. "Art—"

"Art, art! Don't prate about art." Maud did not intend to spare the knife. "Art must be an individual expression and your play is simply hash seasoned with reminiscences. Oh, dear, dear Wallace, you can write a good play. I know you can, when you will write as Wallace Martin, and not after Sudermann, Ibsen, Hauptmann, Shaw. Look at this act. Wallace, tell me, is there no other way of picturing the gay, irresponsible life than by a costume ball in an artist's studio? Must the *vie de Bohème* always be thus presented? Then why does the lover in a problem play usually have to be a Russian prince in Moujik costume? And the heroine's midnight visit to his apartments! Couldn't you, wouldn't they allow you, to write just one play without it? And need the lady, after her past has been discovered and fully discussed, always go out into the tempest in search of her better self, and slam the door behind her?"

"Maud! Maud! You—you are pulling down the pillars of the temple," gasped Martin. "It's blasphemous! Every one says the play is good. You can not judge from a rehearsal. Let us change the subject," with dignity. "Since you have not hesitated to criticize me, I feel that I am justified in again urging you not to go into these gaudy advertising methods. Willoughby Hewston seems to feel that Cresswell was terribly chagrined at his wife's going into business. And truly, you should urge her to show some consideration for him."

"A fig for Willoughby Hewston." Maud fumbled in her bag and drew forth an envelope. "Here is a letter I got from Cresswell yesterday. He congratulates me on the enterprise we have shown, and says that he is delighted that Dita's interests have found so congenial and healthful a channel in which to flow."

CHAPTER XV

A WIDOW'S SMILE

One morning, a California morning, all sea-breezes and flower-scents and golden sunshine, Mr. Hepworth read, as he ate his breakfast, a letter from Willoughby Hewston. The letter, in itself, was a long one, and it also contained a bulky enclosure. This enclosure was the full page of a sensational New York newspaper. This exhibited enormous, black head-lines, screaming innuendo of the most blasting character. In the center of the page were pictures of Hepworth and a dark, heavy-browed young woman, with large eyes and strongly-marked Hebraic features. The page was further embellished by pen sketches surrounding these photographic reproductions, sketches of a startling and romantic nature, a wrecked automobile, a picturesque young woman in very high heels and a very long coat, fainting into the arms of a tall, rather elderly man, presumably Hepworth.

Hepworth had scowled and reddened at the first sight of this dreadful page, and his expression did not improve as he continued his perusal of it. Finally, however, his face cleared. He folded it neatly together and placed it carefully in his pocket-book. Not a pleasant incident, but closed. No use in crying over spilled milk. This newspaper account of an adventure had occurred nearly nine days ago and therefore any wonder it may have excited was practically over. He turned again to Hewston's letter and re-read it with mixed expressions in which amusement predominated.

When Hewston set out to be profoundly serious, Hepworth always found him intensely funny. Finishing his friend's admonitory epistle, Hepworth next picked up one addressed to him in a smart feminine hand, Alice Wilstead's. He ran his eye over several pages, and then paused at a paragraph which he read over two or three times, his rather worried look changing the while to one of profound dismay, for Mrs. Wilstead not only stated that she was carrying out a long-cherished intention of visiting California with her friends, the Warrens, but, what was more, she was staying not upon the order of her coming, but coming at once.

She digressed at this point to express her pleasure at the thought of seeing him so soon again. He bestowed upon these protestations of friendship one bare, ungrateful glance and rustled over the various sheets of her letter, hoping to gain, if possible, some more definite information; and there it was before his incredulous and resentful eyes.

She was, she explained, writing this "hasty note" (it was eight pages) within an hour of leaving. She expected to arrive in Santa Barbara on the Thursday afternoon train. Why, Great

Heavens! He clattered his coffee-cup impatiently in the saucer. This was Thursday morning and he had made all arrangements to spend a rather diversified day, including golf and a luncheon at Monticito with Fuschia and her father, a little fête in honor of Jim's triumphant return, with "the earth, by George, the earth and nothing less in my vest pocket."

"And Alice," Hepworth clattered his cup again, he knew her of old. She was quite as inquisitive as her delicately-pointed tip-tilted nose indicated, and if he wasn't on hand to greet her, she would make life a burden to him until she discovered why.

Hepworth, however, was used to coping with difficult situations. He took what odds fortune offered him and coldly, nonchalantly played to win. He sat for a few moments in deep thought. He had no intention whatever of giving up his day's pleasuring. The only problem which occupied him was what to do with Alice. Inspiration followed thought. He rang the bell and despatched a hasty request that Mr. Hayward Preston come to him at once.

Mr. Preston was a favorite with all mothers, especially those with daughters. They spoke of him in an almost lyric strain. Naturally, one might expect to find him an egregious ass, and avoided of all men. The wonder is that he was not. He had an agreeable appearance, admirable manners, excellent business abilities. His virtues were all a little obvious and robust, and if one insisted on a flaw, it might be said that he lacked subtlety. So much the better. Subtlety destroys a healthy interest in the commonplace and makes of the straight and narrow way a tame and monotonous pathway too rocky for speed.

"Preston," said Hepworth with his usual courteous charm when this younger associate in certain business enterprises appeared, "I wish to ask you a favor, or, to put it more correctly, I am going to do you a favor. I have just received a letter from an old friend of mine, Mrs. Wilstead, saying that she will arrive this afternoon on the three-thirty train. Unfortunately I have another engagement and can not meet her at the station, as, under other circumstances, I should very much wish to do; so," with another cordial smile, "I am hoping that you will be free to act as my proxy."

Mr. Preston was not free. He had something else on hand, but this fact he did not hint by so much as a flicker of an eyelash, relegated it to the background of his thoughts to be settled later. He was not letting any opportunities to do "the chief" a favor slip lightly by him.

"I shall be very glad to meet Mrs. Wilstead, if you can assure me that she will accept me as your proxy," he said with a frank smile. "Let me see. The afternoon train. And how shall I know the lady?"

"I will send my chauffeur with you. He knows her. You are sure, Preston," solicitously, "that this does not interfere with any of your plans?"

"Quite sure," returned Preston with convincing sincerity.

"Thank you," said Mr. Hepworth devoutly; he made a mental vow to the effect that Preston should never rue this day.

Thus, it happened that Alice Wilstead, on stepping from the train at the conclusion of her trip across the continent, found, instead of her old friend, a good-looking young man awaiting her, a young man after her own heart, with that gravity and stability of mien, and the dependable smile, which, being in strong contrast to her own volatile self, always impressed her pleasantly.

Hayward Preston, on his part, gazed at the most attractive woman he had ever seen, of the type he particularly admired. Tall, graceful, her vivacious irregular face lighted by the gleam of white teeth and the sparkle of dark eyes, the air of the great world clinging about her as lightly as a perfume.

To her joy, this delightful, wholesome-looking, grave man stopped before her. "Mrs. Wilstead?" he asked.

She looked at him and smiled. It was the most effective smile in her whole arsenal reserved only for very special occasions.

"Mr. Hepworth was at the last moment detained by certain business matters which are holding him a prisoner at his office and he asked me to act as his proxy. This ought to identify me, ought it not?" with a smile, and he gave her the card upon which Hepworth had written a few lines.

She barely glanced at it and then smiled again, the same smile, only a little diluted. She had seen at once that it was strong wine for Preston.

"You must meet Mr. and Mrs. Warren," she turned to the two who were fussing over their luggage. Warren was a tall, good-looking man and his wife an amiable, attractive little person.

Preston left the question open to them whether they wished to go to their hotel at once or would prefer to drive about, and see something of this new world, into which they had just stepped, and they decided in favor of the latter suggestion.

Through the town they drove, exclaiming over the roses, along the palm-lined boulevard by the shore and then in a rash moment at Alice's request, they turned toward the mountains. A rash suggestion and one that Preston had cause to rue, for presently they passed a carriage being rapidly driven in another direction and all apparently in the highest spirits. It was a party of three, two men and a girl, a slender, tanned, laughing girl, who caught Alice's eye at once. The next glance revealed the man who sat beside her, and who was leaning toward her explaining something, to be Cresswell Hepworth. As Alice bent forward, doubting the evidence of her senses, this girl lifted a bonbon from a box on her knees and held it out toward Hepworth with a pair of tiny gilt tongs. He snatched it deftly in one bite, to the accompaniment of immoderate laughter from his friends, in which he joined.

Oh, dignity! Oh, austere grief! What crimes are committed in thy name! In these days one might well paraphrase the famous lines from *The School for Scandal* and render them: "When a young girl marries a middle-aged man, what is she to expect?" The situation was graver than even Willoughby Hewston could have predicted. In the first surprise Alice had exclaimed, "Why, that's Cress!" And then to relieve Preston of embarrassment before the Warrens, an embarrassment which was manifesting itself in the deep flush which overspread his face, "He probably got through sooner than he expected," she said in a matter-of-fact tone and dropped the subject.

But she thanked fortune that both Mr. and Mrs. Warren were talkative people given volubly to voice their enthusiasm over the beauty about them, and thus her rather stunned preoccupation passed unnoticed.

She had upon her journey, and even before she started, pictured herself as a sort of missionary, with the not altogether unpleasant task before her of cheering up poor Cresswell. She knew the strength of his few affections, his devotion to Perdita and therefore she had some idea of how deeply this breach between them had affected him. But like most women, even the experienced ones, she had never realized that the masculine and feminine attitude toward grief is as wide apart as the poles. They may both wear rue, but with a difference. Woman seeks a cloister that she may brood over her sorrow, commune with it, hug it to her heart in solitude, but man does his best to shake that black, haunting shape, tries to lose it in a crowd, and willingly sips any kind of a nepenthes which seems to offer him forgetfulness.

Alice Wilstead had not expected that Hepworth would make any unmanly exhibition of his woes, weep on her shoulder or be excitingly dramatic; she knew him too well. But she had expected to see him a little older, perhaps; a little grayer, sadder, more quiet, with a hint of melancholy in his eyes. He might—occasionally she pictured the scene—open his heart to her now and then in a grave and reticent way and disclose a strong man's grief; but instead she had seen him sitting up in a very smartly appointed carriage beside a correspondingly smart young woman in a white serge gown, who was in the very act of popping an enormous *marron glacé* between his willing teeth.

"Men," said Mrs. Wilstead to herself, with cynical humor, "are all alike." A nugget of wisdom, by the way, which frequently falls from the lips of a sex prone to generalize from a personal experience.

On arriving at the hotel, Mrs. Warren professed herself a bit weary and retired to her rooms, followed by her dutiful husband, but Alice Wilstead, afire with repressed curiosity, suggested, with another of those smiles, full strength now, that Mr. Preston take a cup of tea with her. She was more tired than she had thought.

For a few moments, Mrs. Wilstead spent herself in enthusiasm for the beauty and charm of the place. Such air! Such scenery! Such flowers! Then she was solicitous about Preston's tea; two lumps of sugar and two slices of lemon? What mathematical exactness! She took a sip of her own. Just the right strength and of excellent flavor. What interesting looking people at the table over there; she believed, no, she was quite sure that she had seen them, perhaps met them before. Yes, she remembered the daughter distinctly. It was in Switzerland, a year ago. She was completely absorbed in the scene before her. "Look at that absurd man yonder, Mr. Preston." Preston eagerly fell in with her mood, lulled to a false sense of security. Then without a minute's warning she opened fire.

"A charming young woman," she began, "is a much more plausible, less hackneyed and convincing excuse than a 'pressing business engagement.' I'm surprised Cresswell did not think of it. But that would be telling the truth, and you men avoid that as much as possible in dealing with women, do you not?"

"You have taught us that you prefer the other thing," he returned with some spirit, although his soul quaked within him.

"Who is she?" asked Mrs. Wilstead, without preamble.

"I don't know," said Mr. Preston miserably. He knew perfectly well that Mrs. Wilstead was too experienced to believe him, and would scorn his clumsy subterfuge. This confused him frightfully, but he hadn't the faintest idea what else to say, so he stumbled on with what he felt was yokel-like stupidity. "Really, I do not know."

"No, of course you would not know under the circumstances." Mrs. Wilstead's tone was sweet and sincere, but beneath the sugar-coating of innocence he discerned the bitter pill of her complete understanding. His ears burned and felt the size of an elephant's. He was very unhappy. He stirred his tea round and round, as if his spoon were an egg-beater.

"Now that you are here," he said awkwardly, "she will be heard of no more."

Although he never knew it, that speech advanced him leagues in Alice Wilstead's favor. The genuine sincerity of his tone would have warmed the heart of any woman standing with reluctant feet where the brook of *passé* joins the river of middle-age.

Alice regarded the opals on her fingers (she was born in October) with a pleased yet humorous smile.

"Accepting your inference, what chance has an elderly widow against a young and lovely actress?"

Preston started. She had played trumps when he was least expecting them. "Then you know—" he said.

"That Miss Fuschia Fleming is a star that will shoot madly from her sphere to brighten the firmament of New York this spring."

"I supposed, of course, that was her game," he said soberly. But he was thinking not so much of Fuschia Fleming as of that after revelation which this delightful woman had made. A widow of charm, of sparkle, of money. One felt the latter. She unconsciously exhaled it. And best asset of all, the old and valued friend of Cresswell Hepworth. Preston was no cold-blooded schemer, neither was he an ardent, impetuous Hotspur. He merely calculated chances, not only by virtue of temperament but training, and when this jewel of a chance flashed its dazzling rays, he instinctively estimated its weight, the accuracy of the cutting and possible value.

Therefore Mr. Hayward Preston made such hay in the next few minutes, that when he left, or rather when Mrs. Wilstead dismissed him, he received another of that particular brand of smiles and walked home with his head among the stars.

CHAPTER XVI

FATHER AND DAUGHTER

One morning, shortly before she left for New York, Miss Fuschia Fleming and her father sat in the sitting-room of their suite in the hotel at Santa Barbara. The sunshine without lay broad and white and dazzling. Within it seemed to be reflected, although through many tonal shadings in subdued, but still golden points of emphasis. There were bowls of yellow roses, there were baskets of oranges and lemons, there was Fuschia herself in a morning gown as pale as the gold of her hair which looked paler than ever in contrast to a great tawny, orange-colored flower, which she had leaned from her window and plucked a short while before and thrust carelessly above one ear.

Her chair was completely surrounded by newspapers, colored supplements, Sunday magazine sections. They billowed about her like waves. Whoever would reach her must cross a crackling sea. On the opposite side of the room, her father reclined comfortably in a large easy chair, smoking an excellent cigar and poring intently over a page of "past performances," with pencil in hand poised above it.

"Goodness!" said Fuschia suddenly, "she's a dream!"

"Who?" asked her father, looking up.

"Mrs. Hepworth." Fuschia was gazing at a page which presented many pictures of the same lady. "Put down that dope sheet, papa; it's time wasted studying it. All your money is needed to back just one favorite, and copper just one bet, and that's me."

"In common with my brothers, men, the workers and the shirkers, I am always ready with advice," obediently laying aside his paper.

"Save it for the weak brother then. I want to talk to you, to clear out my own thoughts. Now Mrs. Hepworth—"

"Cress' wife?" her father interrupted with a show of interest. "What's the matter there, Fuschia? Why isn't she here?"

"She's got a mission in life, just like you and me," Fuschia showed her beautiful even teeth in one of her widest, curliest smiles. "Yours, with the great motto inscribed upon your banner, 'Home-keeping youths have ever homely wits,' is to rescue your brother from the deadly thraldom of the home; mine is to reform the stage; Mrs. Hepworth's is to redeem women's clothes. She has all kinds of theories about color and design and she wanted to put them in practice. That nice Mrs. Wilstead says that she's an odd, capricious, undisciplined creature, but a genius in her line. Oh, I've learned a lot about her from what Mrs. Wilstead and all these newspapers have told me, and what Mr. Hepworth hasn't told me. Papa, dear, I never admired any one in my life as I do that man. I've tried every way but using a drag-net to get him to tell me the whole story, but he's stood every test. He'll talk freely on any other subject."

"Didn't happen to give you any inside talk about those Arizona properties, did he?"

"He did not. You see he married the poor but beautiful girl, and then she got playing too gaily with Eugene Gresham, the great artist. You've heard of him surely. It was the triangle, you see. Same old dramatic motive. Then suddenly, just as every one was standing on their tiptoes to enjoy the view, why the triangle flew to pieces. The Cresswell Hepworth part landed

138

out here, the Eugene Gresham part went to Europe, the Mrs. Hepworth part went into business with a Miss Carmine, and opened a big establishment in New York, and every one came down on their heels with a thud, and are still staring at each other wondering what's doing."

"If Cress really wants her," remarked Fleming, flicking the ashes from his cigar, "he surely wouldn't be such a fool as to leave the field. He'd stay and fight for her."

"That's man-talk," said Fuschia lightly contemptuous. "A crazy idea you all have, that you can make women love you. Don't you know how the leading man always walks about the stage clenching and unclenching his hands, and muttering, 'By heaven, I'll make her love me; I'll win her against all the wir-r-rld.' Poor souls, they think they can dazzle us into loving them; and many feel that if they only talk enough about themselves, and their great achievements, what they've done and what they're going to do, that they can't fail to fascinate us; and it often suits us to let them think so. Awfully funny, isn't it?"

"I never succeeded in fascinating 'em, no matter what line I took," said her father with feeling.

"Women don't care much for you, do they? Well, cheer up, Daddy, dear. They've never loved me. Once in a while, they're very nice to me, and we purr and purr and rub noses, but all the time we are watching each other out of our green eyes, and then one day there's the swift stroke of the velvet paw and the deep mark of claws."

"Mighty little purr and velvet for me," Fleming's petticoat reminiscences were invariably gloomy, "mostly claws."

Fuschia's unfeeling smile curved nearly up to her eyes. "How is that Idaho property anyway?" she asked with apparent irrelevance.

"Fine, my dear, fine. I think Cress may really make something on it himself, but in any event, he'll have no difficulty in unloading it."

"I'll need a pile of money for my campaign." She took an orange from the basket and began tossing it from one hand to the other. "I've brought a good deal of study to bear on the arrangement of this checker-board. I always like to get on to the game just as much as possible. Why have I been traveling about with those miserable little stock companies putting up with all kinds of hardships? Just to get experience. Now I'm ready for New York!" She mused a moment, and then took up the subject with fresh enthusiasm. "It's helped me a lot, all this newspaper notoriety about myself and Mr. Hepworth. Puts me before the public as nothing else could. Just look at these pictures!" She plunged her hand down into the rustling sea, and held out a Sunday supplement to him. "There's a lovely picture of the auto tumbling over a cliff and me landing in a tree. Simply great! Now just as soon as I get to New York, Mrs. Hepworth's got to be a sister to me."

"How do you know she'll cotton to you?" asked Fleming.

"What's that got to do with it?" His daughter opened her eyes in surprise. "I need her, for through her, I mean to have my portrait painted by Gresham. And his prices! La, la! Sure, you can put your hands on real money and plenty of it?"

"Fuschia, my child," her father laid aside his "dope sheet" and bent impressively toward her, "this new proposition has more in it than even you can spend, and you know what that means. It's one of those spectacular properties that make a poet of a man. You can talk it beautifully, splash on the color, you know, and it writes as well as it talks. Shows up superbly in a prospectus, photographs like an artist's dream. Just the thing to capture the eastern imagination. You see, it matters very little whether the property is intrinsically all right or not. That is always problematical, and to be left in the hands of Providence. The great thing is to know what is going to capture the eastern imagination. That's what you're really dealing with, not the proposition itself, by Jingo, but the eastern imagination."

"That's just what I tried to tell that unborn babe of a press agent this morning," cried Fuschia, nodding her head in emphatic agreement. "I got him because he was a Mayflower Yankee, just out of Harvard, and yet he's got no more idea of how to deal with his own people than a new-laid kitten. He came bounding to me an hour or two ago with a lot of stuff he'd been working over nights with wet towels around his head and a pot of black coffee at his elbow.

"'I think I've struck it,' said he. 'It is both true and new!' Pop, it was like this. 'Miss Fuschia Fleming can really do things, therefore she does not waste time talking about them. One of the most competent of stage managers, she never loses her temper. Admirable self-control a striking characteristic. Thoroughly systematic and methodical.'

"Lord, Papa! I felt sorry for the kid. It like to killed me, you know. Well, I waited a bit till the daze wore off and then I said, 'I'm sorry, honey, but it won't do. If I'd made good in New York and had 'em all rooting for me, it would be different, but they're effete Easterners, boy, used to ruts and routine, and you can't change their breakfast food on 'em like that. They won't stand for it. Give 'em the same good old press notices that mother used to make back in 1860. Don't talk about my "trim neatness." You won't believe it, Daddy, but the poor kid actually did that! I said, 'Say that my favorite house costume is a Mexican riding-suit hung with silver dollars, and that, in cold weather, I always wear a Navajo blanket over my shoulders. Have a sketch of me rolling a cigarette between the thumb and second finger of one hand and throwing the lariat with the other. Describe me, when only fifteen, playing Rosalind in the redwoods of the Yosemite before a wildly enthusiastic audience of miners and cowboys. Then say that once before, when appearing before the most brilliant audience ever assembled in a San Francisco theater, I became so overwrought that I began to shoot holes through the drop curtain.' Do you think that was all right, Papa?"

Her father gazed at her with an almost awed admiration. "Honest to God, Fuschia," he said at last, "I don't know what to think of you. Here I've spent my life handling those Easterners, singly and in bunches, and here are you, without either experience or training, on to the game intuitively. Fuschia, this is a proud day for me. I've never told you, little girl, but sometimes I've had my doubts about your bringing up. I tell you after your mother ran away with my best friend and then divorced me for desertion and shortly died, leaving you, a two-year-old girl baby to me as a last bequest, it was a black hour. Like one of those Bible boys—Peter, wasn't it?—I went out and crew bitterly. 'If she was only a boy!' I said. 'What can Jim Fleming do with a she thing like this?' Then I took another look at you, in your white dress and blue shoes, smiling at me with your mouth all over your face, and, true as I stand here, Fuschia, you were the first thing in skirts that didn't seem to be looking at me across a great gulf.

"And then I talked to myself a while. You see, if your mother had come to me as man to man and said, 'Jim, I'm tired of you and I want to marry Henry,' I'd have said, hard as it might have hit me, you know that, Fuschia, 'Kate, I don't blame you, and I'll do what I can to help you.' But she preferred the feminine

142

route, a note on the pincushion and she gone with all her jewels and ten thousand I'd given her to buy a diamond necklace. But as I say, I looked at you in your white dress and blue shoes and that friendly grin on your little mug, and I said, 'God knows how it'll work, but this girl thing here ain't going to grow up thinking that there's fences built all around her and that she's got to coax and sneak and pretend to get her way. Poor Kate! With great price she obtained her freedom, but my little Fuschia, here, she's born free.'"

"Good old Poppy-doppy!" Fuschia's tone was fondly approving and something like a tear glimmered in the depths of her turquoise eyes. "I'm glad you never tried the snaffle bit of parental training and home influences on me, because I'd sure have kicked myself free, and it mightn't have been pleasant. But to come back to the present, Mr. Hepworth is so splendid, that unless his wife is really in love with this boy-Raphael or whatever he is, I'm going to get into the game and make home happy for the Hepworths."

"Cautiously, cautiously, daughter," admonished Fleming, looking a trifle alarmed. "That's all right on the stage; but in real life when an outsider tries to join the parted hands of husband and wife, he's likely to get a cuff on the ear."

"Oh, men are crude," sighed Fuschia. "You didn't suppose I was going to do the child at Christmas act, did you? No, what I mean to do, that is, if it's just her imagination and not really her heart that's captured, is to take her boy-Raphael away from her."

Fleming gasped, and, lowering his head slightly, looked at his daughter from under his eyebrows. "Fuschia," he said, "there are few things that can feaze me. 'No limitations and no limits' has always been my motto, but you do, child, you really do

143

take my breath away sometimes. Why, if report is true, Cress' wife is one of the most beautiful women in the world."

"Um-huh," Fuschia yawned indifferently. "What has that got to do with it? I've usually," she continued thoughtfully, "succeeded in getting anything I wanted; that is, men. The wildest of them will trot right up to me, and eat out of my hand."

"You're your father's own little girl, Fuschia," said Jim with emotion.

"Yes, and it's a good thing I inherited father's constitution as well as his spell-binding abilities, considering that I have to be practically my own press agent, stage manager and all the rest of it; the management of Fuschia Fleming and Fuschia Fleming herself and then take up the task of reuniting families besides. But Mr. Hepworth is a good, good man, Papa, and we're going to make him happy, even if we have to do it on his money."

CHAPTER XVII

DO YOU LOVE ME?

The Warrens and Mrs. Wilstead had remained in Santa Barbara a week, time enough for Alice to discover that Hepworth was in no apparent need of the consolatory offices of his old friends, that Fuschia Fleming was a most entertaining young woman, and that Hayward Preston's attentions were persistent and his intentions manifest and purposeful.

During the next month, no matter in what part of the state they were and in what hotel Alice and her friends registered, Preston was sure to turn up before the day was over; and to begin at the earliest possible moment his unending argument. Along palm-shaded boulevards, under avenues of pepper trees, in orange groves, on lonely mountain trails, in the shadow of old missions, on surf-pounded beaches, in secluded nooks of great hotels, everywhere and at all times he told his plain, unvarnished tale. He had now asked Mrs. Wilstead to marry him in every resort in California; and had not yet succeeded in winning her consent, and the day of her departure was drawing near. Within two days she would be leaving for New York. It was at Pasadena that Mr. Preston made his last desperate stand.

He and Alice were strolling about the gardens of the hotel; she had not wished to get too far away from the sheltering Warrens, and there Preston was making what he assured her was his last appeal.

She, however, preferred to view his condition of mind and heart in a psychological rather than a sentimental way.

"It is a habit, an obsession," she asseverated, tilting her rose-lined parasol toward the sun so that charming pink reflections fell upon her face. "You have lost sight of the object in the zest of pursuit. It is the game which absorbs you, believe me. The winning would disconcert you. Yes, it's the game. I am convinced that you have lost sight of the goal and all that it entails."

Mr. Preston merely looked at her. "It entails you," he replied simply.

"It entails a great deal more," her speech was as quick as his was slow. "You are, you tell me, exactly thirty-three years old. I, Alice Wilstead," she shut her lips and breathed hard a moment and then gallantly took the fence, "am just thirty-eight."

Not by even the flicker of an eyelash did he show either surprise or dismay. Alice's heart went out to him. She really adored his impassivity; it was so unlike anything she was capable of.

"What has that got to do with my loving you and your loving me?" asked Preston stolidly.

"Everything," she answered deeply, regarding with drooping eyes and wistful mouth a great, fragrant rose which she held between her fingers. "If we could but hold this moment, if neither of us would know further change, why—"

"Then you admit that you could care for me, that you do care for me," he exclaimed with brightening eyes.

"Let it remain at 'could' and 'might,'" with one of her swift smiles. "But under any circumstances, I do not wish to marry any one. Look at my admirable position, rich, free, supposedly attractive, young—a widow, you know, is always a good five or six years younger than either a married or an unmarried woman. One is regarded as a young widow until one is quite an elderly person. Now, really, why should I marry?"

"There isn't any possible reason," agreed Mr. Preston unhappily, "unless you love me, and then there is every reason. But are you not tired walking up and down, up and down these paths? Shall we not sit down on this seat a few minutes?"

She acquiesced. It was a glorious morning and the spot was enchanting with all this fragrant, almost tropical plant life blooming and blowing about them, and Alice, impelled by the softness and sweetness of the air and scene, forgot her adamantine resolutions and lifted her eyes to his in one long and too-revealing glance.

"Alice, Alice"—there were all manner of tender inflections in his usually colorless and unemotional tones—"you can not now deny—"

"Yes, I can," she cried quickly; "I can and I do. Hayward, believe me, it will never, never do. You are looking at the matter from the man's viewpoint, I, from the woman's, and, in cases of this kind, the woman's is the surer, the more safely intuitive."

"Bosh!" Preston's exclamation was calm, but pregnant.

"But consider, consider," she besought him. "Look at us, you are the robust, ruddy, phlegmatic type that will not change in twenty years, and I am exactly your opposite in every respect and that's the reason you like me and therein lies the whole tragedy. I'm nervous, mercurial, emotional, and nothing, nothing brings wrinkles so quickly as vivacity and expression."

"But you haven't any wrinkles."

"Not yet. Care, massage, a good maid and a light heart have kept them at bay. And, oh! gray hair!"

"But you haven't any gray hair," he said, with the same patient obstinacy.

"Not yet, but when they do begin to come, they come all at once. Hayward, I do not deny that I could care for you if I would let myself, but when I realize that for a woman to marry a man younger than herself makes life one long, hideous effort to keep the same age as her husband; oh, it is too frightening! Just think! No matter how much one may long for repose to have to be always up and exercising to keep one's figure; to have to hold on to one's complexion by always sleeping in stifling masks and slippery cold cream; to be always watching the roots of one's hair to see if it doesn't need retouching, and, worst of all, to have to be gay and vivacious and conceal, heaven knows, what twinges of rheumatism under a smiling face."

"You're just talking," said Preston calmly. "Keep on if it amuses you. It doesn't mean anything at all to me. Not at all." His success in life was largely due to the fact that he always kept the main object in view and never permitted himself to be diverted by side issues. "Your personal appearance ten years from now has nothing to do with the matter. We may both be dead ten years from now. There is only one question to be discussed and that is, 'Do you love me?'"

The petals fell from the red, red rose as Alice twisted it nervously in her fingers.

"I think I have given you ample proof of my liking for you," she said at last, "but the *loving* is obscured in doubts."

"Forget them, for my sake," he murmured. "Can't you, won't you, Alice?"

"If I could only get away from those mental pictures," she confessed. "They stand between us like a barrier. Just think of arriving at the point where you want to doze after dinner and dream over some nice, slow, old book, with your head comfortably nodding now and then. And the fire flickering and the cat purring on the rug. Lovely, isn't it? And instead, think of realizing wearily that you've got to spend the evening at the opera or playing bridge. And that, of course, means turning yourself at an early hour into the hands of your maid for repairs and decoration. And then you've got to sit upright the whole evening because your stays, which are guaranteed to give you the lithe and willowy figure of youth, will not let you lean back. And you do not dare to smile, because you will crack the kalsomining on your face; neither may you move your head, you are so afraid that the curls and puffs and braids may not be pinned on tight. Oh, it's a dog's life!" she sighed heavily.

"And it's not for you," Preston spoke firmly. "There is nothing coltish about me." Alice laughed, it was so true. "Business is all that very deeply interests me, and amusements bore me very much. I like the after-dinner doze and the fire and cat already. You will probably have more of that kind of thing than you like, if you marry me. Alice, will you not consider?"

"Mrs. Wilstead, Mrs. Wilstead," a page's voice rang through the shrubbery and came nearer and nearer and Alice took from him a thick letter addressed to her in Isabel Hewston's hand and adorned with a special delivery stamp.

"From a dear friend," Alice exclaimed. "Will you excuse me while I look at it? There may be some matter of importance, you know."

149

In Preston's manner there was no hint of his annoyance. He behaved as well as a man could when interrupted in the most fervent declarations of affection which the limitations of his nature permitted him. He even suggested that he withdraw, and rose, hat in hand. Could complaisance, consideration go further? There were only two days before him, and she had never been so near yielding before.

"Oh, no, no," almost possessively, she stretched forth a hand to detain him. "You have nothing to do but wait, and I shall run through this," touching the letter, "in a moment."

Preston sat down beside her again and lighting a cigarette, smoked and looked out over the brilliant garden before him while she read.

It was evident, Alice discovered this before she had finished the first page, that Isabel Hewston was actuated by no deeper motive than pure, erratic impulse when she placed that special stamp upon the letter. At least so Alice and Preston probably would have agreed and Isabel reluctantly would have admitted it. But the Fates who sit in the background and transmit wireless messages to mortals would have smiled inscrutably and shaken their heads. If Isabel hadn't stuck that stamp on for no reason whatever, and if the page hadn't sought Alice through the breeze-caressed, rose-scented garden and given her the missive at the exact moment he did—but, as Eugene Gresham would say, "What's the use? Why conjecture?" What really occurred was this:

"Dearest Alice," wrote Mrs. Hewston, "how I envy you in that southern paradise while here the weather merely changes from sleet and snow to rain and then back again."

There was a page or two of this and of Willoughby's various ailments and symptoms, and then a long and glowing account of her visit to Perdita Hepworth, and a great deal of minute, enthusiastic description of the gowns that Dita was designing for her.

This Alice read with interest, but greater interest still did she bestow upon the statement that there appeared to be a coldness between Wallace Martin and Maud Carmine, owing, it was said, to the fact that she had ruthlessly criticized his last play, and prophesied accurately its speedy failure.

"It does seem too bad, dear," Isabel wrote next, "that you, away off in California, should have to come in for your share of the gossip which seems so sadly rife this season."

Here Alice clutched the pages and, bending over, bestowed upon them an almost breathless attention. What could Isabel mean?

"It is perfectly stupid, of course," the letter ran, "and I would not think of mentioning it to you except that we have always been frank about such things, and, anyway, you ought to know. There is a rumor about that you went to California hoping to catch Cresswell's heart in the rebound. People now believe that he and Perdita have definitely separated and that you knew this, and, as some one put it to me, so vulgarly too, dear, camped down on his trail. They say now that the incident of the actress was merely to make things easier for Perdita in gaining her freedom, but that soon after that is granted her, Willoughby says that, as those coarse men express it, you will lead Cress to the altar."

"Darn Willoughby!" Alice breathed hard as she muttered the words between her clenched teeth, the vivid scarlet of hot anger suffusing her face. Preston turned quickly to her, throwing away his cigarette, and ceasing to regard the brilliant garden through meditative, half-closed eyes. "What is it?" he asked. "Something has worried you."

"No," she smiled, with an effort, and shrugged the matter lightly off her shoulders, "some mistake about a very trifling matter. It annoyed me for a second, that is all."

For a moment or two neither spoke. Alice was watching the flight of a butterfly that soared in the air until almost out of sight and then came back to drift about a group of tall, white yuccas.

"Hayward, do you still love me as much as you did ten minutes ago?" She smiled charmingly at him, that very, very especial smile of hers, and he, with his rather slow perceptions quickened by love, read capitulation and a real affection in her softened eyes.

"Hayward, do you love me?"

"Alice!" And the depth and fervor of his love will be appreciated when it is recorded that he, Hayward Preston, the most conventional of men, deliberately tilted her rose-lined parasol and in the face of the world and before the very eyes of an advancing couple, kissed her.

CHAPTER XVIII

PLAYING THE GAME

It was only a day or two after her arrival in New York that Fuschia Fleming, who had been rehearsing the greater part of the night, opened her sleepy eyes in the hotel chamber to find her maid bending above her with a visiting card in one hand and a perplexed expression upon her face.

"I hated to waken you, Miss Fuschia," she said, "but when I saw the name—"

"What is the name?" Fuschia's voice was drowsily indifferent.

"Mrs. Cresswell Hepworth."

"*Mrs.* Cresswell Hepworth!" Both indifference and sleepiness were things of the past. Miss Fleming sat up in bed with a spring. "She's in the parlor, isn't she? Here, Martha Mary, hustle about. Get me out my gold-colored kimono with the silver wistaria on it, and some yellow stockings and slippers. Tell her I regret having to keep her waiting, late at rehearsal last night. You know the proper thing. Now, go ahead and do your prettiest and then dance back here and help me get into things."

"Certainly no time wasted," reflected the actress standing before her mirror, winding her long ash blonde hair round and round her head. "I dare say it's a case of 'Gur-rl, what have you done with me husband?' There is only one reply to that. I shall draw myself up haughtily and say, 'Pardon, Madame, it was you who first carelessly mislaid him, not I.' Where the deuce are my hair-pins? She'd never come to my apartments with a cat-o'-nine-tails under her golf cape, or a bottle of acid in her shopping bag. Sure-ly not. They always choose the foyer of the theater for such stunts. Oh, Martha Mary," as that person whom Jim Fleming had once designated as a "vinegar-faced-Sue" returned to the bedchamber. "I can find nothing. Everything has crawled under the bed or the bureau. How is the lady dressed for the part? Handsome, dark garments, rich, dark furs, black veil over face, handkerchief handy?"

"The lady is wearing rose-colored cloth and chinchilla," replied Martha Mary literally.

"Rose color and chinchilla. That is a note out, positively frivolous. Oh, dear me! I am only half put together. You get more worthless every day, Martha Mary. Put on all my moonstone rings, for luck. They may save my life."

When Fuschia entered her temporary drawing-room, Perdita Hepworth was standing with her back to her, gazing from the window out upon the bleak wind-swept streets. March was departing with lion-like roars and buffets and striving bravely but vainly to obscure his ugly countenance in clouds of dust. Hearing a slight sound, she turned and saw advancing down the pleasantly warmed, flower-scented room, a young woman whom she instantly likened to a pale but radiant ray of spring sunshine.

This sunshine, yellow kimono, pale yellow hair, a cheek like the heart of a tea-rose, gold-colored silk stockings and slippers, paused between a jar of white lilacs and a basket of hyacinths. The lion-like roars without seemed suddenly all hollow pretense. Spring had come to New York and involuntarily Perdita smiled in greeting.

"Miss Fleming, please forgive this unseemly early call; but you see it is important, this matter I wish to see you about." Perdita thus opened the conversation.

"She can chew up the scenery about me husband all she wishes," said Fuschia to herself, "if she just lets me look at her. Her pictures give no idea of her. She's red roses and music and emotion. She's poetry and romance. My Lord!"

In spite of Perdita's brave attempt, conversation languished. She appeared to be weighing some matter which lay on her mind. At last she looked up with a slightly ironical smile. "You will think I have come on some affair of state, Miss Fleming, the way I am hesitating—"

Fuschia here made a violent mental protest. "Now don't you begin by telling me that I broke up your home, because I didn't. You broke it yourself."

Mrs. Hepworth made an impatient gesture as if at her own unusual lack of adequate expression.

"Do you play cards at all?" she asked, "bridge or—"

Fuschia could not suppress one stare of surprise. "Play bridge!" she murmured, wondering what that had to do with the matter. "No, I have no card sense. Strange, too, for papa has a lot."

"The reason I asked was this," in rather diffident explanation; "I was wondering if you could appreciate what it means to make an unexpected play which takes several tricks—to play trumps in such a way as to make the other players gasp with surprise, to—"

"Oh, I know what you mean," said Fuschia comprehendingly, a light dawning in her puzzled eyes. "You are talking about playing the game. Why, of course, I understand. That's all there is; that's what I'm on this dizzy old planet for."

157

But although a basis of mutual agreement and understanding was thus established, Dita seemed still to struggle with an unwonted embarrassment.

It was not, however, within Fuschia to prolong a situation of this kind. She bent forward, her elbows on her knees, her fingers covered with moonstone rings clasped lightly in front of her, her eyes full of a thousand twinkles and the upturned corners of her mouth curving almost to her eyes.

"Let's get down to cases, Mrs. Hepworth, man to man. Is it a go?"

Perdita drew a breath of relief and smiled back. She certainly was not one of the few, the very few, who could resist the twinkles in Fuschia's eyes.

"It's a go," she answered; "then man to man, it is this way. You have made it easy, you see, for me to say the things I wanted to, although I did not know in what feminine phrases I might have to clothe them. But you and I are, at present, very much in the public eye. Now every one is waiting to see what our attitude toward each other will be. It is assumed openly by the newspapers, as you probably know, that there is a sort of woman's war on between us. Now, Miss Fleming, I want—"

"Your husband," supplemented Fuschia mentally. "Well, I haven't got him; never did have him; don't want him."

"—to design your stage costumes and to have it so announced," concluded Perdita.

Then she saw a remarkable change come over the dainty, thistledown Miss Fleming. Her mouth became an almost straight line, the gleam in her eyes was almost uncannily shrewd. She gave Perdita's words a concentrated consideration for a few moments and then nodded two or three times, brief, quick, clean-cut little nods.

"Great!" she said succinctly. Then her mouth curled again, the twinkles, like splintered diamonds, came back to her eyes. She flew across the room and threw her arms about Perdita, enveloping her in a momentary and rose-scented embrace. Her enthusiasm was unrestrained. "The advertisement is above rubies," she cried. "No wonder you are such a success."

"Oh, that is no credit to me," replied Dita carelessly. "I have a sort of sixth sense about clothes, you know. It is my one gift. I know the moment I put eyes on any one exactly how she, it is always she, of course, ought to look. I see colors when I look at people. Women often say to me, 'Oh, I can not wear this or that color,' when it is just the one thing they should wear, it is their mental correspondence."

"And how are you going to dress me?" asked Fuschia with intense interest.

"Principally in gold and silver," Dita answered without hesitation. "You have on the right thing now. Most designers would put you in black, because you are so very fair. They would try to make you striking by force of contrast, but not I. You see very few women of your coloring could stand the dazzle of gold and silver. It would completely eclipse them; but you are mentally dazzling. Your personality is strong enough to reduce anything you wear to its proper place. One must take all those things into account in designing, you know. Now you are quicksilver, sunlight, glimmer of day on speeding waters, and we must accentuate that fact; not ignore it and slur it over."

"It sounds fascinating," said Fuschia. "How sweet of you to do this for me."

159

"For myself, you mean." Perdita rose. "You'll do, my dear. You're new, you're different. New York will be yours whether you can act or not."

A flame went over Fuschia's face and seemed to pass as swiftly as it had come; but instead, it remained, focused in her eyes.

"I can act," she said briefly, "and, look here, New York may accept me on the magnificent advertising I've had and will continue to have; or New York may accept me on the strength of my wonderful gowns designed by Perdita Hepworth. That's all right, that's as it should be. But I'm going to make New York forget my press notices, and your gowns and Fuschia Fleming, and I'm going to make it sit tight and still in its boxes and orchestra chairs and balcony seats and laugh and cry with the heroine on the stage who shall be the realest thing on earth to them for the time. That's the game for me, Mrs. Hepworth. That's all the game I care a hang about."

"Maudie," said Perdita to Miss Carmine, an hour or two later, "I have just secured a new commission, a big one."

"What?" asked Maud with interest.

"Hepworth and Carmine are to design the costumes that Miss Fuschia Fleming will wear in the repertoire of society dramas in which she will appear after two weeks of Shakespearean rôles. Paula Tangueray, Mrs. Dane, you know the lot of them."

"Perdita! The cheek of her. To make such a request under the circumstances."

"Maudie! The cheek of *me*," mocked Dita softly.

160

"You!" astonishment was beyond all bounds now. "You!"

"Yes. Did you fancy—" there were those deep vibrations in Dita's voice which always bespoke some strong emotion, "that I was going to endure the spectacle of Miss Fleming triumphant 'in our midst,' and every one watching to see how I would take it, and predicting that only one course remained open for me and that was with dignity to ignore the incident? Not so. The world will see, and this, amusingly enough, happens to be a fact, that Miss Fleming and Mrs. Hepworth are excellent friends, that Mrs. Hepworth is one of Miss Fleming's warmest admirers, and that she, still speaking of myself, has assisted in Miss Fleming's unparalleled success in New York by designing for her some of the most wonderful costumes ever seen on the stage."

"Unparalleled success!" scoffed Maud. "It is rather early to predict that. New York is like a cat. You never know which way it will jump."

"It will jump Fuschia Fleming's way," replied Dita confidently. "You haven't met her."

"Is she so beautiful then? As beautiful as you?"

"Oh, no," Perdita was smoothing out her gloves on her knee. She shook her head decidedly. "Nothing like. She isn't beautiful at all. She's just a slender creature with rather colorless *blonde cendre* hair and blue eyes."

"Oh," Maud was plainly puzzled. "Then what do you mean?"

But Perdita only smiled. "Have you and Wallace made up yet?" she asked with what appeared to the other woman striking irrelevance. "Impertinent, I know; but there's a reason?"

161

"No-o-o," said Maud reluctantly and evidently wondering if Dita had suddenly lost her mind.

"Then do so at once," advised her business associate. "Do so before he meets Fuschia Fleming."

"From what you say." Miss Carmine's chin was high and haughty. "I see no cause for alarm."

"No?" Perdita tapped the table with her finger-tips, still inscrutably smiling.

Maud rarely permitted herself to become angry, but she did so now. She had never imagined that Perdita could be so aggravating. "Just because Cresswell lost his head about her, you think—" she flashed out.

"He didn't," cried Perdita not with bravado, but with a confidence which Maud realized with surprise was genuine. "I hadn't been with her three minutes before I knew that. But take my advice," again her voice fell to that teasing note. "If you really love Wallace make up your differences with him to-day, to-day, before he, a playwright, meets the actress. Then get a new steel chain, one that he can't chew through, and fasten it securely to his collar."

162

CHAPTER XIX

HE CALLS ON HIS WIFE

Early in April Hepworth returned to New York. It was a gentle, smiling April, inclining more to laughter than to tears and striving to obliterate the memories of March. He arrived one evening and wasted no time in communicating with Perdita. The next day in fact was marked by the passage of notes between them, severely businesslike, and yet models of courtesy.

The result of these diplomatic negotiations was that Mr. Cresswell Hepworth, at a suitable hour the following morning, wended his way to his wife's business establishment.

It was a deliciously balmy morning, the rare sort of a day that slips in now and then between April showers and sets one dreaming of the glory of the spring in the silent woody places. The great, roaring canyons of brick and stone floated in a silvery, sparkling mist, and in that atmospheric alembic dreary perspectives assumed an unsubstantial and fairy-like beauty. The little leaves on the trees fluttered in the soft breeze and were so young, so green, so gay that they lifted the heart like tiny wings of joy.

In spite of himself there was the hint of a smile about the corners of Hepworth's mouth and this deepened and deepened until as he rang the bell of his wife's door, he suddenly became conscious of it, and carefully suppressed it.

The sphinx, past mistress of inscrutability of expression, would have paid him the tribute of a flicker of admiration as he entered the reception-room. It was without a suggestion of curiosity or even interest in his eyes that he glanced absently about him; perhaps the long droop of the lids at the corners,

163

which appeared to accentuate his rather weary and listless gaze, was more marked than usual, but this was always so when he was making mental notes and registering his observations with the rapidity and accuracy of a ticker.

He awaited Perdita in her reception-room, that charming apartment, and here, in view of certain events which occurred later, it would be well to give the plan of the first floor.

This room opened from the hall and ran the length of the house with windows at the front looking out upon the street while those in the rear opened upon a strip of garden. There was another door at the lower end of the room, which, with the long room, formed an ell, and terminated the hall.

Dita kept Hepworth waiting a bare moment. Her approach was unkindly noiseless, but nevertheless he heard her, and was on his feet, his eyes meeting hers full as she appeared in the doorway. The conventional banalities of greeting were gone through with ease on his part, grace on hers.

Merciful banalities! They gave him time to consider the change in her, a change which was to him sufficiently striking almost to have trapped him into an expressed surprise, and this change was so subtle that he wondered that it should yet be so apparent. It was not a matter of outward appearance, that remained the same in effect. It was a mental change so animating and vital that Cresswell felt all former estimates of her crumble. Had she always been so, and had he never really seen her until now? Had time and absence in some way cleared his obscured vision? He felt a momentary sense of confusion, a brief mental giddiness, and then he pulled himself together. The first impression was the correct one. She had changed, and thereby had gained, gained tremendously in poise.

But there was no time now in which to analyze impressions.

"So this is the magic parlor where all the ugly women are transformed into beauties." He looked about him as if he had not thought to glance at her surroundings before. "The presence of mere man here seems rather profane, do you not think so? Ah, well, my stay is brief. You have proved, haven't you, that it is not an impossibility after all, to paint the lily and gild refined gold?"

"So few women have any taste," she said carelessly. "And oh, their houses! You should see them when I go over their hideous houses like a devouring flame and ruthlessly order out all their dreadful junk. And the most awful objects are always the most precious in their eyes. I feel so sorry for them. I have always a guilty sense of being a naughty boy robbing a bird's nest, and the poor mother birds stand around and flap their wings and hop and shriek. It's very mournful, but they needn't have me if they don't want me."

He laughed. "And Maud? Is she, too, well and happy?"

Dita lifted her hands and eyes. "That is a very tame way of describing her. Her gowns are dreams this spring, she is considered almost a beauty; people, you see, are gradually forgetting that she was ever 'that plain Maud Carmine who plays nicely,' and Wallace Martin and herself are engaged to be married." A faint, amused smile crept around her mouth at this announcement.

Hepworth looked up with sudden interest. "Indeed! Well, that might have been expected, I dare say, but will it not rather seriously interfere with the business?"

"No," she shook her head. "No, I think not, Maud has no intention of quitting. Wallace's plays are more or less

165

problematical and Maud has invested a good deal of her money in this. It is really paying remarkably well, you know."

"Dita," his voice was low, and he could not conceal the chagrin, the touch of pain in it. "Why have you never touched a cent of your own money, since my departure? I only learned a few days ago that you had not. I can not begin to tell you how it made me feel. It not only distressed but deeply wounded me."

She twisted a little in her chair. "It—it has never been necessary," she said. "We began to make money at once. Really, Cresswell, Maud and I have prospered beyond our wildest dreams."

"But suppose you had not. Is your prosperity the only reason you have not touched it? Would you have done so under any circumstances? That is what I have been asking myself for the past week, and am now asking you."

She flushed uncertainly. "Ah," she said. "I can not answer you that. I can not tell. One never knows what one will do when the pinch comes."

He smiled faintly. "I'll not put any more embarrassing questions to you, but confine myself to perfectly safe topics. You are looking very well."

"I am well."

"And happy? But there, that is hardly a safe topic, is it?"

A sudden light came into her eyes, making them warm and softly bright. She smiled at him with a fresh, almost childlike enthusiasm. "Yes, I'm happy," she said, "happier than I've ever been in all my life. Why, Cresswell, it's been fun, fun. There's been lots of work, and lots of planning, but nevertheless, I've never enjoyed anything so much in my life. Often I go to bed at night tired out, but it's always with a comforting sense of satisfaction. It's all so varied and interesting, you know, but it isn't that that makes me happy." She clasped her hands and looked up at him with an unconscious appeal for sympathy and understanding in her eyes. "It's better than that, better than anything else. It's meant success, think of it, success. Not a horrid, little picayune one either, but a nice, big one."

He leaned forward and looked at her curiously as if he really saw her for the first time.

"Why, Dita," he exclaimed, "has it meant so much to you as that?"

"Indeed, yes." There was ardor, fervor in her answering exclamation. "I can not tell you how much. I believe I was really morbid on the subject. I believed in failure as a real atmosphere always encompassing me. I had all manner of superstitions, beliefs about it. I believed that with all my strength and youth and energy, I was yet doomed by fate to a tomb of inaction. I seemed so futile, so ineffective. With a restless, active brain I accomplished nothing. You see that was such a dreadful experience, my attempt to earn my living before I married you, and I was so ignorant and inexperienced of every condition of life in which I found myself, that it prevented me from striking out boldly, from believing in myself. So I made the fatal mistake of beginning small, and began to paint all those wretched little articles, and it wasn't my *métier* at all, Cresswell, really it wasn't, so, naturally, I failed. And," as if it had suddenly occurred to her, "I have found it so interesting to dress Miss Fleming. Designing her costumes has been fascinating."

"That was a very wonderful and a very clever thing of you to do, Perdita." There was a tone in his voice she did not understand. She began to praise Fuschia and he leaned back in his chair listening. She could see the mere gleam of his eyes between his almost closed lids. She wondered if he had really heard one word she had said. In reality he was bestowing upon her such attention and study as he had never dreamed of giving her before. She felt, however, in spite of his apparent indifference, that he was so far in sympathy with her, that she was impelled in spite of herself to continue her confidences.

"Do you know, Cresswell, it's a horrible thing to be considered a beauty. Oh, you may laugh," he could not help his mirth. "I know beauty is supposed to be the heart's desire of every woman; but there are many drawbacks. Every one, without exception, takes it for granted that you are a fool. Your sense is always considered in reverse ratio to your good looks, and then, it's such an uncertain thing. Just when you need it most to console you for the disappointments and disillusions of life, it departs, and horrid things, wrinkles and gray hairs, take its place."

"Perdita! What an absurd creature you are!"

"Ah, Cresswell," her tone was pensive. "You have always been successful. You can not imagine what failure feels like, that deadening, hopeless sensation." She was vehement enough now.

"Can I not?" At last he lifted his drooping lids and looked straight at her. "My dear Dita, I can give you cards and spades on every emotion of failure you have ever felt. I recall one case in particular, where I failed so conspicuously and brilliantly, that I am overcome with surprise at my own stupidity every time I think of it. But as you have been talking that case has

168

reverted again and again to my mind, and it has struck me that there is still a chance that I pursued the wrong tactics."

She drew back wounded. He had then, as she had once or twice suspected, not been listening to a word she said, and how his cold face had glowed at the mere thought of retrieving a business blunder.

Hepworth got up and began walking about the room. "And Gresham, what of him?" he asked presently, breaking the silence which had fallen between them.

"He is quite well, I believe," she was furious at the conscious note which crept into her voice, at the scarlet which flew to her cheek, but one thing she had never been able to endure and that was any evidence of cowardice in herself. She lifted her eyes bravely to his and held them there. "He has been in town since January," she said. "I have seen him very often."

"Ah, painting as brilliantly as ever, I dare say? A genius, Eugene! Unquestionably."

Again silence fell between them, and lasted until she broke it with the constrained question: "Are you—are you going to be here for some time now?"

"No, I shall have to be in London more or less during the summer, but I have some matters which must be attended to first. By the way," as if struck by a sudden thought, "what are your plans for the summer?"

"I have made none. I have not even thought of such things yet. I dare say I shall go somewhere for a bit of a change, but," with a smile, "business is so very brisk."

He laughed and took one or two more turns up and down the room.

"Dita, do you remember that I told you once that you were a remarkably clever woman? Well, I merely wish to call that fact to your attention, and reiterate my statement. Oh, I must tell you, I have a new amulet, a wonder. I will tell you the history of it when you have more time. You have the case in your keeping have you not? And the tray with the one empty space?"

The blood rushed to her face. "I have the case," she said coldly. "It is locked in my safe here. Do you wish it now?"

"No," he shook his head. "Wait until I bring the amulet. May I bring it late Wednesday afternoon? And why not dine with me then? Say you will, Dita. Give the world something to talk of, something to puzzle over." She had never seen him so eager.

She hesitated a bare second. "I will. Yes, I will be very glad to," but lifting her eyes to his: "Are you so sure that one of those amulet trays has an empty space?"

"It had when I last saw it." His voice was unreadable.

"But that is months ago; perhaps you will think differently when you see it Wednesday evening."

There was a flash over his face, which vanished as quickly as it had appeared. He drew nearer to her as if about to speak, then apparently reconsidered the intention. "I really must not keep you longer," he picked up his hat. "Of course, there are a number of matters to be discussed, but they can wait. We will reserve them for Wednesday evening. Good-by." He held out his hand. She placed hers in it.

"Good-by," she returned.

CHAPTER XX

THE MAGIC WORD

"Maud," said Dita, walking in upon that young woman, a package of letters in her hand, "a lot of things are happening. Here is a letter, among other things, from Mrs. Wilstead. She says that she is just back from California, and that she needs stacks and stacks of new clothes, and wants our designs. It will be fun dressing her. She is so extremely good looking."

Maud stirred restlessly, frowned, bit her lip, but did not speak.

"Just back from California," went on Dita. "I wonder—I wonder, Maud, if she could possibly have come on with Cresswell?"

"Very probably," said Maud. "In fact, I think nothing could be more likely."

"Why, what do you mean by speaking so mysteriously?" Dita widened her eyes. "Suppose they had? Nothing, after all, could be more natural."

"Nothing, I suppose." Maud was trying hard to be non-committal. "But let her go to some one else. If we take any more people, we shan't get away this summer. We have more on our hands now than we can manage. Yes, let her go to some one else."

"But, Maud," Dita hesitated, "I really think we should refuse some one else and take her. She is an old friend."

"Old fiddlesticks!" cried Maud impatiently.

"Maud! What is the matter with you? A touch of spring fever? Really, I think we must consider her."

"But if I ask you not, Dita"—there were almost tears in Maud's voice.

"But why should you ask me not? This is too bewildering."

"Ah, well," Maud spoke now with the calmness of despair, "since you force me to tell you, I ask you not because Mrs. Wilstead has been constantly with Mr. Hepworth in the West this winter, and the current gossip is that he is only waiting for a divorce to be arranged between you and himself, to marry her."

There was silence for a moment on Dita's part. Her eyes were downcast, mechanically she sorted the letters in her hand. "Then what of the talk about Fuschia Fleming and himself?"

"Oh, they say that she took a back seat when Alice Wilstead appeared on the scene. But really, Dita, this move on Alice's part makes me furious. The idea of her being guilty of such wretchedly bad taste. I have always liked her, been really fond of her, in fact, but this crass exhibition of bad breeding disgusts me. I dare say that she doesn't care so long as she gets results; that is, the benefit of your taste and skill to enhance her waning beauty; but look at the position it is going to place you in, Dita. For number one to design the trousseau for number two is really too absurd. It simply goes beyond all belief. Dita, you must, indeed you must, write her the curtest, coldest of polite notes and tell her that we are entirely too busy to consider her."

"Very well. I'll humor you so far," returned Perdita. "What is it?" turning to a maid who entered with a visiting card. "Ah, Eugene! I asked him to come this morning. I particularly wanted to see him and I don't want you present. There, don't get that stony look of despair on your face, Maudie; think how good I have been all winter, only seeing Eugene once in a blue moon, and then in your company."

"But I want you to keep on being good," pleaded Maud; "especially now."

"I am gooder than you can possibly imagine," laughed Perdita, "but, all the same, I do not wish you tagging about this morning." She smiled teasingly at her puzzled business partner as she left the room.

She went down to meet Eugene in the same room at the same hour she had talked with her husband the day before.

But Eugene was not one to endure for one moment a situation dominated by the shadowy third person. No woman should gaze at him with the remembrance of yesterday in her eyes, the smile of wistful reminiscence on her lips. An hour with him must be a dazzling and kaleidoscopic episode. He would hold it in his hand, and at the bidding of his will, the moments, like bits of colored glass, should revolve and melt and mingle— rainbow arabesques on the background of Time.

"Your meditations, remembrances and regrets for your oratories, my dear," his challenging eyes seemed to say, "but with me you live, you laugh, you thrill responsive to the harp of life; the yesterdays forgotten, the to-morrows unborn."

"Dita!" he caught her hands in his as she entered. His eyes were shining, his head thrown back. He was more vivid than the spring sunshine which fell through the open windows.

"Eugene! You look as if you had just received some wonderful new commission."

"So I have, a commission to love you. That is right, blush. Dita, why do you not always wear rose color? But no, don't listen to me. If it were blue or green, I would be making the same request. Dearest, my eyes drink in, drink up your loveliness. You never, never were so beautiful as you are this morning."

"Eugene, you are mad; too foolish for anything. What is the matter with you?"

"Mad doesn't half express it. May I smoke?" He took her consent for granted, for he was already rolling cigarettes in his deft, supple fingers. "Yes? No? I am delirious with joy. Hepworth is back as, of course, you know. That can only mean one thing; every one says that just as soon as a divorce can be decently arranged, he and Alice Wilstead will be married. The verdict of the world is that he was so angry at your going into business that he flung off to the West. It was the most spectacular of your many caprices and it proved the last straw for him. Blessed last straw!" lifting his eyes devoutly. "And then Alice Wilstead cleverly appeared on the scene and the consoling offices of friendship did the trick."

"Three months ago it was Fuschia Fleming, according to gossip." Her eyes were downcast, her tone expressionless.

"Oh, that," he blew rings of smoke lightly through the air and followed them with gay eyes; "that is a part of the game. That was making evidence for you. It is all arranged that I am to paint her portrait, you know. I have not met her yet, either." He threw his cigarette through the window. "Dita, Dita, how can you sit there so cool and still? When I think that you are actually on the very eve of freedom, I become delirious with joy."

"So sure of the winning, Eugene?"

"Dita!" His face clouded, there was a world of reproach in his voice. "That is a terrible trait in your character, that teasing desire of yours always to fling a little dash of cold water on one's mounting enthusiasms."

"There is another dash coming," she laughed. "I want my amulet, and I want it at once, to-day. I know," anticipating his protestations, "that you returned it to me the afternoon Hepworth left for the West, and I would not see you to receive it in person. Then, my mind was so perturbed and occupied that I didn't think of it again before you sailed, and since your return," a little smile creeping about her mouth, "I haven't thought about it either; but now that the matter has come up between us, please see that I have it to-day, Eugene."

He had looked slightly annoyed while she was speaking, but now he bent toward her with his most charming manner, his most winning smile. "You know my greatest weakness, Dita? I try to overcome it, really I do," in laughing excuse, "but in spite of will or reason those superstitions of mine persist. Alas! They do." He admitted it as a naughty little boy might admit a passion for stealing jam. "And I have tremendous faith in that old charm of yours." He picked up another cigarette from his skilfully rolled little heap, placed as orderly on the table beside him as if they were his paint brushes.

"Ever since I have had it," he went on, "the luck of the high gods has been mine. Princessin, Contessin and high Altessin still clamoring to have their portraits painted. The critics amiable and almost intelligent, money pouring into my coffers and pouring out faster than it comes in—I wish there were such a thing as a money-tight purse—and best of all, ah, best of all, the love of my heart so near, so near." His eyes held the warm glow which changed, irradiated them. "The star of my life comes slipping, wavering through the spaces of the sky and down the purple pathways of heaven to my arms." He leaned forward quickly and almost enfolded her.

"Eugene!" She stood haughty and tall before him. "You assume entirely too much. You have from the beginning. More, much more, than I have ever given you any reason to assume. According to the tradition the amulet can only bring one luck when it is given with the heart's love; and I never gave it to you, Eugene, never. You laughingly filched it one day when I took it off the chain about my neck, that you might look at it more closely. And you are so sure, so sure of me, when I am anything but sure of myself. I have never deceived you as to the state of my feelings. How would that have been possible when I am still so doubtful myself? Ah, those doubts!"

"They are nothing, dearest, nothing. I shall brush them away as I brush cobwebs." He put his hands upon her shoulders and stood gazing deeply into her eyes.

"Ah," she shook her head, and, at the same time, stepped away from him, "I am no more sure that I love you than I was six months ago."

"Never any more sure?" His voice deep and rich as a low-toned bell.

Her black eyelashes lay long on her cheek, where the crimson, the hue of a jacqueminot rose petal, was spreading. "There are moments," she admitted, "times when I am with you that I believe that the magic word has been spoken and that my heart has blossomed in purple and red, that I truly love you, but," she shook her head sighingly, "the moment I am away from you, I know that that is not so; that you haven't said the magic word yet, 'Gene."

"But I know it, that magic word," he whispered, "and I shall awake you, just as the Prince did the Sleeping Beauty. Not with a word at all, dear, but with a kiss." He bent forward, but she had slipped away from him, and before he knew it had put almost the length of the room between them.

"You—you must not talk so to me now, 'Gene," the words were barely breathed, "and," with a desperate clutch at a safe topic, "my amulet. I must have it by to-morrow morning."

There was a flash like fire in Gresham's eyes. A quick scowling change darkened his whole face. He picked up the five or six beautifully rolled cigarettes which yet remained of his neat heap and tossed them out of the window.

"I see it," he cried harshly. "You probably have Hepworth's box of amulets in your keeping. You wish to return it to him, and show him when you do so that your old charm is safe in its place. Oh, I can see the whole scene. He will courteously hand it to you and say, 'Your property, I believe, my dear Perdita.' I can hear his frigid, formal utterance. And you will accept it with that grand, ancestral manner of yours, murmuring, 'Thank you, yes, I regret that I can not ask you to accept it as a small contribution to your collection, but that being out of the question on account of certain traditions which adhere to it, I feel that I must continue to hold it in my possession.' Why not be honest, Dita, and tell him that you have given it to me?"

"Eugene, you are impossible. You go entirely too far." There was no mistaking the displeasure in her voice, and his immediate recognition that it was cold, not hot anger, brought him to himself at once.

"Flower of magnolia!" his voice fell to all those exquisite and heart-touching modulations of which he was master. "I was only teasing. Forgive me. You shall have your bit of glass early to-morrow morning. And until I see you again I shall dream only of the wonderful, beautiful years we shall have together. We shall wander about the world, here, there and everywhere, and I shall paint the glory and color of the universe and you, always you, Perdita, the focus, the center, the heart of all beauty."

CHAPTER XXI

TWO ANNOUNCEMENTS

Dita had barely finished her breakfast the next morning when the message was brought to her that a lady who refused to give her name but insisted on seeing her at once upon important business awaited her in the reception-room.

Dita hesitated a moment, debating whether or not to rebuke the maid, who must have yielded to the lure of gold so readily to forget her orders, and send back a peremptory request for the lady's name and her business, or whether to yield to her natural and feminine curiosity and grant an interview to this visitor who appeared so desirous of maintaining an incognito.

This brief hesitation proved a loss, however, to the waiting lady, whose method of being announced showed that she hoped to take Perdita by surprise, for Maud Carmine entered at the moment and with some show of indignation in both voice and expression informed Dita that Mrs. Wilstead was the person guilty of strategic entrance.

"Such impertinence!" breathed Maud. "Scrawl a note in pencil, Dita, to the effect that it will be impossible for Mrs. Hepworth to see Mrs. Wilstead. That will show her that her ruse and her bribes have been quite unsuccessful."

In her ardor for Mrs. Wilstead's demolition Maud had forgotten that the last thing Dita could endure was dictation. Now, no sooner had the words of admonition left her lips than, to her chagrin, she saw Dita's chin lifted, Dita's nostrils quiver, Dita's shoulders flung back ever so slightly.

"I think I shall see her." Mrs. Hepworth was on her feet, her voice cool, firm, pleasant, with just that little warning vibration which always meant danger. "You may tell Mrs. Wilstead that I will see her immediately." Her eyes scorched the maid, who hastened to obey, with the impression of an X-ray having been turned on her immaculate white waist, and exposing with startling vividness the crisp, green bill hastily thrust within.

"Come, Maudie," Perdita touched her on the shoulder in passing. "Do not look so downcast. Why do you wish to deprive me of a little legitimate amusement?"

Maud, strong now in tardy wisdom, said nothing, and Perdita's light, quick step might be heard a moment later descending the stairs.

Alice Wilstead turned hastily from her contemplation of the small green yard without the window.

"My dear Perdita!" She came forward with Dita's note of the day before in her hand. "I just received this in the morning's mail, and I lost no time in getting here, I assure you, and making the attempt to see you by hook or crook. I know it's outrageous of me, but I don't understand, and I want to understand. Why is it, my dear, that you have refused to take me? Surely I'm not a hopeless case." She smiled ingratiatingly, and Dita was bound to admit that never had she appeared more attractive. Her piquant face was radiant with happiness, the whole effect of her was of a sort of buoyant joyousness.

Dita's chin was just half an inch higher than when she had left Maud, her smile was sweet and cold and faint, as remote as if it had been bestowed upon a passing acquaintance in Mars, and she remained standing.

Mrs. Wilstead's mental recoil was but momentary. Her cause was good, her motives pure, her courage high. Above everything, she desired the benefits of Perdita Hepworth's genius. They were on sale, to the high bidders, and she did not purpose to be excluded merely because it was to be supposed that she would espouse the cause of her old friend, Cresswell Hepworth, in the event of open differences between himself and his wife.

"I regret, Mrs. Wilstead," Dita's voice matched her smile, "that it will be quite impossible for us to take any one else now. The summer is almost upon us, you see."

Mrs. Wilstead should not be blamed for not seeing. April, as wind and sky portended, was about to burst, not into tears, but into a snowstorm. Alice shivered in her furs.

"Oh, but, my dear child," she begged, "do have some mercy on me. Here am I getting my trousseau. Oh, no wonder you start. I've always said that I never, never either would or could do anything so idiotic as to get married again, and yet here I am not only considering it, but actually committed to a wedding-day. And that is to be so appallingly soon. I tried and tried to put it off a little longer, but he is so impatient."

Dita's mouth had frozen, and the haughty and incredulous gaze which she cast for a brief, indignant moment on Alice would have turned one less bubblingly gay into a pillar of salt. This interview seemed incredible. She had always regarded Alice Wilstead as an especially well-bred woman, but this greed to attain an object at the sacrifice of her self-respect, even decency of feeling, and regardless of the position in which she would place the woman with whom she pleaded, was, to Dita, shocking, insulting, unforgivable. While she waited the fraction of a second to command her voice, Alice spoke again.

"But you seem angry." She was obviously both hurt and bewildered. "What have I done? Surely, you will not fail me now at this most crucial moment of my life. Why, consider, I am going to marry a man five years younger than myself."

Dita caught at a chair, and sat down, the room seemed to whirl about her, she pressed her hand to her brow.

"Alice Wilstead," she said, "what on earth do *you* mean?"

"I mean what I say," returned Alice with a touch of acerbity. "I am going to be married. What do you mean?"

"But to whom, to whom?" Dita was all impatience.

"To whom? Why, to Hayward Preston, of course. One of your husband's business associates in the West. Surely you knew that?"

"I wish I had Maud by the throat," muttered Dita irrelevantly.

It was twenty minutes later when Maud put her shocked and disgusted head within the door.

"Dita," coldly surveying the two enthusiasts before her, who sat together in jocund amity, "Mrs. Hewston is out here in a state of great perturbation. Do you wish—"

But she got no further, for Mrs. Hewston, in the superiority of her greater bulk, pushed Maud into the room before her and now stood, the picture of pink and white and plump tragedy, on the threshold.

"Oh, Alice, I am glad to find you here," she wailed, advancing further into the room, while Maud discreetly closed the door, not upon herself, oh, no, but behind both of them. "You are always such a support." She sank into the chair Dita pushed toward her. "It's Willoughby, of course." She drew her handkerchief from her bag and mopped her eyes.

"Perdita Hepworth," she abandoned her spineless attitude and sat upright, speaking with vehemence. "I am more ashamed of being here than I can ever make you understand. But Willoughby!" There was resignation in her uplifted eyes, acidity in the purse of her mouth. "He is the dearest, most lovable fellow in the world," she looked at her listeners suspiciously, but meeting no correction, permitted her irritation a natural outlet, "but he is the most obstinate, stupid mule the Lord ever made."

"What is it now, dear?" asked Alice sympathetically.

"This, and it's quite enough," returned Mrs. Hewston bitterly. "Cresswell Hepworth, your husband," accusingly to Dita, "and may Heaven forgive him, for I never can! dined with us last night and just before he left, Willoughby got to asking him about his plans and Cresswell was telling him that he was due in London before long. 'But how much longer will you be in New York?' asked Willoughby, and Cresswell said, with a queer little smile, 'I can't quite say. There are a number of things to be looked after, among others a duel I may have to fight.'"

The women looked at each other in pale horror. Dita herself ghastly, half rose from her chair.

"I told Willoughby," sobbed Mrs. Hewston, "that it was just one of Cresswell's jokes. You know that odd, dry humor he sometimes shows, but," despairingly, "you also know Willoughby. He tore and snorted and raved and routed all night long. I would rather have had a hippopotamus in my room. And he excoriated you, Perdita. Called her the most dreadful names, really," this to Alice and Maud, confidentially

184

and quite as if Dita were not present. "He said that Cresswell's life was ruined because of the caprices of an ungodly, wanton girl. Yes, Dita, I don't blame you for being angry, but it was worse than that, too. You see, he's got the idea firmly into his head that Cresswell is going to fight a duel with Eugene Gresham and—"

"For goodness sake, let us keep our common sense," said Mrs. Wilstead, laying a detaining hand on Dita's shoulder, noting that Mrs. Hepworth's eyes were turned longingly toward the telephone. "You know perfectly well, Isabel, you know, Maud, and you, also, Dita, that Cresswell Hepworth does not for one moment contemplate anything so crazy. Nothing could induce him to put either himself or you, Dita, into such a position. Such a thing would be entirely against his nature. He would regard it as farcical melodrama, turn from it even in thought with infinite contempt and scorn. The idea of Willoughby thinking such a thing. Just like him. Meddlesome idiot. Ah, I don't care, Isabel, you know he is one. I wish I had him here now."

"He's out there in the motor," wept his wife. "He was afraid I wouldn't come and tell Perdita unless he came with me. But, Alice, you shan't speak of him so, he's the best—"

"He's still there," interrupted Maud, who had gone to peer from the window at Mrs. Hewston's announcement that this watch-dog of Dita's morals waited without, "with his head out of the window looking up at the house. And, oh, Heavens!" falling back against the lintel, "here is Eugene Gresham coming up the steps, and Mr. Hewston is glaring at him until his eyes are standing out of his head. He is purple in the face. Now he is speaking to the chauffeur. Why, they are off, gone like the wind."

Mrs. Hewston fell back limply in her chair. She seemed incapable of speech for a moment. "Alice," she said at last, in awe-stricken tones, "he has gone to tell Cress that Eugene Gresham is here."

"Well, what of it?" snapped Mrs. Wilstead. "Cresswell will only laugh at him and smooth him down. You know that."

"I hope so," breathed Mrs. Hewston. "He seems to amuse Cresswell. Fancy. But then," more understandingly, "he doesn't have to live with him."

CHAPTER XXII

HEPWORTH MISUNDERSTANDS

Dita's fears calmed by Mrs. Wilstead's essentially common-sense point of view, her confidence was further restored by Eugene's evident ignorance of any plots and plans on Mr. Cresswell Hepworth's part of bringing this triangular situation, involving himself, his wife and the other man, to a fiction-hallowed and moss-grown conclusion.

It was therefore without particular apprehension, at any rate apprehensions of the kind nourished by Mr. Hewston, that she dressed for the dinner *en tête-à-tête* with her husband. It was rather with a sense of mounting interest, even excitement.

She wavered in her choice of a gown, scanning with hypercritical eye a dozen or more. White savored of a school-girl simplicity and disarmed her if she chose to be subtle. Blue was unbecoming; sufficient taboo. "Green's forsaken and yellow's forsworn," she murmured ruefully. Black remained, thin, soft-falling gauze, distinguished, distinctive, exquisite in

186

design and effect; above its shadow rose her neck of cream, her hair was the dusk shadow of copper, her eyes were darkly brilliant.

She hesitated at jewels. He had given her so many. Which would go best with her gown? Then she turned away from even the mental contemplation of them with a feeling of distaste. She could not, even to please him, wear his jewels when he and she were almost strangers, when but the details of their final parting remained to be settled. And yet would it not look a bit odd to appear without any ornaments whatever?

She considered the matter a moment, and then smiling a little, she opened the box which Gresham had given into her hands that morning, and which lay upon her dressing-table.

She turned over this old trinket in her hand, and gazed at it, forgetful of the passing time. How impressive Eugene had been when he had returned it to her!

She gazed at the old trinket.

"I am only lending it to you, remember that, for you will give it to me with your heart's love, Dita, and soon."

She was roused from her reverie by the sound of a motor stopping without. Her maid waited to place a black and gold wrap about her shoulders. "One moment," said Dita. Quickly she slipped the amulet on a thin, old-fashioned gold chain and fastened it about her throat. Then she went downstairs to greet her husband.

Commonplaces of the most conventional and banal order they talked. Nothing else on the drive to the restaurant, nothing else on first taking their seats at the table on one side of the great garish room. There were many curious eyes on them, necks craned, the incredulous whisper ran:

"Mr. and Mrs. Cresswell Hepworth actually together! What does it mean!"

The stereotyped babbling went on intermittently, until dinner had been ordered and the earlier courses come and gone, and then Dita suddenly awoke to the fact that her husband had taken the conversation into his own hands and was actually talking to her. Oh, of course, he had often talked to her before, arranged new amusements for her, discussed what jewels she would like, what plays she would care to see, what people interested her most, what journey she would enjoy.

But now, she almost caught her breath at the surprise of it, he was talking to her as if she were a man, or at least an intelligent human being and not just merely—a pretty woman.

He was talking straight ahead, discussing business matters, several interesting problems which had come up in his affairs during his recent western sojourn. He did not pause to explain anything to her, quite took it for granted that she would understand. He did not apparently stop to consider whether she was interested or amused, and that pleased her enormously. She began to ask questions, and he answered them fully, even pondering some of them carefully before replying. One he considered for a moment or so and then said: "Do you know, I had not thought of that before, that puts a new phase upon the whole situation." Her strand of rubies had never given Dita such a glow of pride and pleasure.

"Ah, why have you never talked to me like this before?" she asked naïvely. "Think of all the stupid dinners we've eaten together when you treated me like a tiresome little girl who had to be continually amused, and I was one, too; as tongue-tied and missish as anything, because you took it for granted that I was."

"No one could accuse you of being either tongue-tied or missish to-night. You are quite matronly in that black gown."

"Oh, I love to hear about the big things that go on," she said enthusiastically, if irrelevantly, "but men will never talk to me about them. All my life, whenever I'd try really to talk sense to a man, he'd say, 'What wonderful eyes you have,' showing that he hadn't heard one word I'd been saying. They always seem to think that I expect them to tell me how lovely I am. It's the curse of the pretty woman."

"Oh, well, console yourself," he said carelessly. "There are prettier women in the world than you, quantities of them!"

"I—I—suppose so." Dita had rarely been so taken aback. She looked at him a moment like some insulted queen. His eyes, however, were discreetly downcast. "Oh, of course," she said as quickly as she could recover her breath, "of course," her laugh was forced and rang hollowly.

"Oh, yes, don't let your beauty get on your nerves. The world is full of beautiful women. My new amulet—I told you that I had a new one, did I not?—was given me by one of the most beautiful women I ever saw. I have her picture somewhere. I must show it to you."

Mr. Cresswell Hepworth was entirely without design in his choice of topics. He had spoken of some of his great western enterprises because his mind had been more or less occupied with them during the day, and had been so surprised and pleased that these subjects had gained his wife's interests that he had continued the discussion of them. Again, in his seeming disparagement of her beauty, he had merely thought to console her for what she regarded as the constant belittling of her mental endowment, evidently a sore spot in her consciousness.

Dita played with her fork a moment without answering his last remark. She had no right to feel either resentment or irritation. Her sense of justice assured her of that, but she suffered a twinge of both emotions, nevertheless.

"Wallace Martin tells me that good old Hewston made an awful scene when those distorted pictures of Fuschia Fleming and myself appeared in the paper." Hepworth laughed more heartily than usual.

"Oh, do not mention that unspeakable old creature!" she cried petulantly. "Tell me of more interesting things."

"Dita," he spoke to her more earnestly, more self-revealingly she felt than he had ever done before, "I am going to tell you something. When I went west last winter, it was not alone because I was called thither by various business affairs, but because, after thinking the matter all over, I definitely decided that the only thing for me to do was to relieve you of my presence. I was convinced that, although you might not be

191

fully conscious of it, still in the depths of your heart you really loved Gresham. I was also convinced that I loved you infinitely, and that it was quite beyond my power to interest you. But since my return I find myself at sea. The moment I saw you I saw the difference in you, the change that made me revise my former crude, stupid estimates of you. I realize that you are the sort of woman who must have an object, a purpose in life, an expression; in fact, that you set little store by the beauty others praise extravagantly, because it has always been yours. You value it no more than one values the sun and wind. It is achievement that fascinates you, isn't it?"

"Ah, yes, but I had failed, you know, and I was afraid to try again. I knew that you were doing big things, but you never would talk of them to me, and I thought that you considered me too stupid to understand them."

"Dita, how blindly we have misunderstood each other. Is it too late?" He whispered the words as he put her wrap about her shoulders, his voice ardent, impassioned as she had never heard it.

She cast one astonished, almost frightened glance upon him. Then, as in a daze, a dream, walked down the room, never seeing the admiring eyes that everywhere met her. She might have been in the desert, as far as they were concerned.

As the door of the motor closed on them a panic of shyness seized her. "You, you spoke of your new amulet," she said, snatching at a topic. "Have you it with you?"

"Yes. But I do not know whether you can get a very good idea of it in these shifting lights."

He took the case from his pocket and, lifting out the ornament, gave it into her hands. It was fashioned of half a dozen uncut diamonds in a setting of the most delicate and exquisite filigree.

"Old Spanish, you see," he said.

"Beautiful!" she exclaimed, turning it over and looking at it more closely. But the attention she was bestowing upon it was a mere seeming. She was thinking, or rather attempting to think, but her heart was fluttering wildly, her whole impulsive nature seemed to impel her to the action she was meditating.

"Cresswell," she lifted a face white as a snowdrop to his, "will you make an exchange with me? Will you give me this amulet and take mine?"

"Perdita!" he cried, "you do not—" his voice broke.

"Yes, I do," she exclaimed, "it is not a wild whim, a caprice on my part. I have been thinking about it all day, ever since this morning."

"This morning!" sharply; looking at her keenly, quickly. "Ah," with a long breath, "it was this morning that Hewston drove poor Isabel to your house to prevent the duel between Gresham and myself." He laughed, but it was dreary mirth. "Hewston is a most imaginative fellow. I have a railway deal on which I spoke of to him as a duel. And so, you were going to sacrifice yourself in order to make quite sure that I would spare Eugene. Oh, rest content, Perdita. He is quite safe from my poignard or pistol. Never fear."

It seemed to her that the satire in his voice bit into her soul. With a great gasp of relief she realized that the car had stopped before her door. "Oh, take your amulet," she cried, "since you will not have mine." She almost threw it at him.

193

He thought that she was angry and sullen as she walked up the steps and into the house without a word to him, and with the barest inclination of the head. In reality, she was striving hard to control her sobs.

CHAPTER XXIII

ITS ANCIENT CHARM

The hour which Dita had set for her appointment with Cresswell Hepworth was twelve the next morning, consequently she was not only surprised but perturbed when Eugene's name was brought to her a little after eleven.

He looked haggard, she thought, as if he had not slept, but his eyes were brighter than usual.

"Good morning, Queen of the May," he cried, coming forward to take both her hands in his as she came through the doorway. "Did you know, by the way, that this is May day? Ah," his eyes fastening themselves on the crystal amulet gleaming against her white gown, "you have it still. That was what disturbed me and drove slumber from my eyelids during the long night. He is a strong man, a very able and masterful man and he wants that amulet and you, Dita, and I feared—oh, you know how things appear in the dead of night, what monstrous and fantastic ideas come to one."

"You might have saved your fears and your fancies," she answered with a delicately ironical smile. "He does not want me. He would, I think, like the amulet. Nevertheless, he declined it."

"Then you offered it to him? Really!"

"Yes," the irony still in her voice. "You were a better prophet than you dreamed, Eugene, you predicted exactly what happened. I offered it to him and he declined." Her voice faltered.

"Naturally," laughing, "what else could he do under the circumstances? Even he, with all a collector's greed, would hardly care for a gift which is supposed to be invariably accompanied by the heart's love of the donor. He knew, poor wretch, that all he was getting was the bit of glass, while the heart's love was mine, for ever and ever mine."

His voice sank to those musical cadences which ever prove so enthralling to the ear. And Dita, who loved music and beauty and romance, smiled dreamily. But doubt, like a shadow, lay in her eyes and about her mouth.

"No," she cried, "oh, I do not know, Eugene. When I am with you, you throw a glamour over me. I believe that I am just on the eve of loving you—that any minute you will say the word which will make me fully realize that I do, but as soon as you leave me, Eugene, the moment passes."

"It is because you are perplexed, worried about this other matter, that is all, dearest. When that is settled and you are free, then I will sweep away at once and for ever all these doubts in your mind, sweep them away as if they were cobwebs."

"Will you? Perhaps," but she shook her head as if only half convinced. "Hush! What is that! I think it was the bell of the outer door. You must go at once, Eugene. Cresswell was to be here at twelve o'clock. It must be quite that now."

"And I have no desire to meet him." He picked up his hat. "I will step through the little back room into the hall, and thence out. I dare say you and he have some final arrangements to make. Is that it, eh?"

She nodded, but without looking at him. Her face had grown very pale and the hand which she placed on the tall back of a chair to steady herself trembled a little.

Her ears had not deceived her, it was Hepworth's ring—and the echo of Eugene's retreating footsteps had barely died away before a maid drew a curtain and Hepworth crossed the threshold.

If he upon his arrival had at once noticed a subtle but marked change in Perdita, she now was struck by an equally vital and informing alteration in him. He had always seemed to her before as one who leaned back in an automobile and merely dictated the directions the chauffeur was to take, but now he was the man who was driving his car himself, at unlawful speed, and keeping quite cool and collected during the performance.

He took the chair opposite the one in which she had seated herself, and she noticed a flicker of a smile across his face as his eye caught the amulet hung about her neck, a tender, humorous, sad little smile.

"Yes, I am still wearing it," she said, as if in answer to some question of his, "and I have had the box containing the others brought down here. It is there on that table in the corner." She spoke with a bravado which only half concealed her embarrassment.

He glanced toward it indifferently. "Then we will fasten my new one in the space left vacant by yours," his swift, delightful smile came and went, transforming his face for the moment like a gleam of sunlight, but although brilliant, it was sad, sad as all regret, and Dita, seeing it, felt some wild, momentary impulse to beseech forgiveness, she could not tell exactly for what.

197

The amulet, her old bit of crystal, was swinging at the end of a long chain, and, a little embarrassed, she lifted it in her hand and gazed at it mechanically, turning it this way and that to catch the different reflections of light.

"Did you know that we are lawbreakers, you and I, Dita?" asked Hepworth with another smile, "meeting to discuss the details of a properly arranged divorce? Well, my dear, it will not rest particularly heavy on my conscience if it makes things easier for you in the least degree. Your lawyers will instruct you just what to do, but there is one matter which I wish to discuss with you personally, and that is some settlements.

"Why, Dita," breaking off sharply and starting to his feet, "what is the matter? Are you ill?"

Indeed he was justified in thinking so. She had grown white as snow. The color had left even her lips.

"No," she spoke with an effort, but she lifted her head, as if by main strength of will. "No," and he was infinitely relieved to see a bit of color creep back into her lips, but the eyes she courageously raised to his were dark with an emotion which he could only translate as fear or horror, he could not tell which.

"Have I offended you, then?" he murmured. "Believe me—"

"No, no," she insisted so definitely that he was forced to believe her. "It was something quite different. Something, something I just remembered."

She was manifestly so confused and disturbed that he did not press the point. It would have seemed both unkind and unwise to do so, and then, although her eyes still retained that curiously shocked, almost horror-stricken expression, the color had returned to her cheek.

"You were saying?" she began, her voice steady enough now. "Oh, yes, I remember, about the money." Those deep vibrations of emotion thrilled her tones. "Well, I won't have it. Won't touch it. I will not hear of settlements. I can make enough for my needs."

He lifted his eyes and looked at her quickly and then the eyelids almost closed. Perdita was under very close observation.

"Naturally, I do not for a moment dispute that. It is a fact already proven, but it is my wish to remove the necessity from you. Your occupation will then continue to be a source of amusement, of interest to you, but you will not feel that it is your sole dependence."

She shook her head with a sort of irrevocable gentleness with which he could not fail to be struck.

"No," she said, "it is really quite useless to discuss the matter. Truly, Cresswell, I will not even consider it."

"But, Dita," he began, then paused a moment as if to make a choice of arguments, desirous of using at once the most potent and evidently preparing to undermine and break down the barriers of her decision if it took a month.

She forestalled him, however, with a quick flank movement. She rose to her feet. "Cresswell," she said, "I promised you last night that I would discuss this matter with you this morning, but now," there was the least hesitation in her voice, "I am going to ask a favor. I dined with you last night, now will you dine with me to-night? Will you? There will only be Miss Fleming and her father, and she will just sit at the table a few minutes, she never dines before playing; Wallace Martin and Maud, and they are going somewhere, so you and I will have the leisure of a long evening to discuss all the pros and cons of this question, your side and mine. Will you come?"

She was looking at him so earnestly, there was something so strange in the depths of her dark eyes, that he felt tempted on the moment to beg an explanation of this postponement. Then, as quickly he relinquished it.

"I shall be delighted to come," he said heartily. "And if to-night you are in no mood to talk over dry details, we will put it off again until a more convenient season."

"No." Her tone was positive. "I am quite sure that we will come to one decision or another this evening. Good-by."

When the curtain at the door had fallen behind him, Dita sat down again. She did not seem to be thinking or mentally engaged in any way whatever. On the contrary, she seemed to be waiting, two or three minutes passed, five. Still she waited. Ah, a bitter smile hovered for one moment around her lips. Her whole tense figure relaxed a little as if the moment which she had so confidently expected had come.

There was the sound of the shutting of the outer door in the small room to the left, then a halting step across the bare and polished floor. Eugene's step. He paused a moment in the doorway leading into the larger room, but as Dita did not turn nor give any sign whatever of having heard him, he came on.

"Back again, you see," he said. "I saw Hepworth leaving the house just as I came about the corner up here, so I knew the coast was clear. May I sit down?"

For the first time Dita looked at him. He was unmistakably not of the same temper in which he had left her an hour before. The buoyancy and spring of him had vanished. His eyes were clouded, his mouth depressed, certain lines on his brow and about his mouth stood out more markedly than usual. In fact, he seemed to have halted midway in some mood between dismay and anger. And as Dita observed this, there again played about her mouth for one instant that same, sad, bitter, secretive smile.

She had leaned back in her chair as if prepared to remain some time, but she made no effort whatever to carry on a conversation or even to embark on one.

The frown deepened on Eugene's brow. This attitude on her part was evidently irritating to him.

"Everything settled, Dita, and satisfactorily?"

"What do you mean by satisfactorily?" she asked, letting a moment or two lapse between his question and her answer.

"I mean everything arranged in your favor," he replied with a short laugh. "He is rather sure to do that, you know. He likes to do things with the grand air."

"Oh, no, Eugene, it is you who like to affect the grand air. With him it is natural."

He looked up at her quickly. "It sounds, it sounds," he said, "as if you might possibly be on the verge of a sirocco. Don't Dita, I implore you. I am off the key myself."

"Why?" she asked.

He lifted his shoulders. "Ah, that I do not know."

"I refused any alimony, Eugene," she said abruptly.

"What! Oh, Dita, you must not! Why, it is the height of folly! My dear child, it is quixotic to the verge of idiocy." All his moodiness had vanished. He was arguing her case fervently enough now. "You have had your head turned by the success you and Maud have enjoyed in this venture this winter, but that is purely ephemeral. You were a fad, a novelty. How long do such things last in New York? And here is Hepworth willing and anxious to endow you with houses and lands. Dita," and never had she heard him plead his love with such fervor, "Dita, you must not ruin your whole life by a blind whim. You must listen to advice. You must be guided by your friends in this matter.

"It is true, of course," he continued, "that I make a very large income, but I lay nothing by. It is impossible. I must keep up an appearance—the painter prince, and all that sort of thing. It is expected of me. It is a part of my stock in trade."

"Then you consider, 'Gene," her voice was calmly, reassuringly reasonable now, "you consider that fully to enjoy life we must both possess more than an ordinarily large income?"

"Dearest Dita," he bent forward with his tenderest, most ingratiating smile, "do not for one moment mistake me. I think, I know we could be happy without a centime between us, but viewing life as it is lived and considering your tastes and my tastes, the mode of existence to which we have accustomed ourselves and all that, I think we, like most other people, would do well to avoid the perilous experiment of comparative poverty. Whether we wish to believe it or not, really to invest life with romance and interest and charm requires more than mere imagination, of which you and I possess an abundant store, Dita. It also requires money."

"It would require a great deal more than that for me, Eugene," she rose to her feet now and stood looking at him as if from mountain heights, so remote and distant she seemed. "Remember the old legend of my amulet,"—she lifted it and swung it to and fro as she talked,—"that sooner or later it would force the one who possessed it to reveal himself in his true character? Well, it has proved its ancient claim. You apparently possessed it long enough for it to force you to reveal your true self; or perhaps that was inevitable under any circumstances."

"What do you mean, Dita?" he, too, had sprung to his feet, and stood facing her, both fear and chagrin in his eyes.

"This," she flung out her hand with the amulet in it; "while I sat here talking to Cresswell, I was turning this square bit of crystal this way and that, watching it catch the light. Suddenly, as I held it between my thumb and forefinger, I saw you, it reflected you quite clearly. You thrust your head a little forward from the door, down there," indicating by a gesture the door at the lower end of the room, "anxious to hear the better what Cresswell was saying and quite sure from the position of our chairs that we could not see you. Then I sent him away and waited. I knew, I knew instinctively, that you would do just as you did, Eugene, and—so I waited. I knew that I should hear that outer door close, that I should hear you walk across the floor, I knew it."

The moments pulsed like heartbeats between them.

"I shall not deny it," he said at last, "but Dita, Dita, I did it for you. I felt that you would follow some quixotic course, which you would regret for a lifetime. I know so well your mad, impulsive recklessness. Oh, Dita," he stretched out his arms to her.

203

There was no responsive movement on her part. She stood mute, immovable, eyes downcast, as if she could not bear to look upon his humiliation.

The long chain had slipped through her fingers, and the amulet swung at the end of it, to and fro between herself and him, like the pendulum of an inflexible fate.

"Dita," his voice was irresistibly appealing, "you will not thrust me thus out of your heart, oh, not for this!"

"You never had a place in my heart, Eugene, I know that now."

She swept across the floor, but as she put up her hand to pull aside the curtain before the door, she paused. "I—I'm sorry, Eugene," she faltered and by an effort of will lifted her eyes to him at last.

But they fell neither on the shamed nor the conquered. His head was thrown back, his eyes met hers. He was smiling, and his smile held unfathomable things. It spoke of a spirit eternally young and yet which had felt the weary weight of all dead and crumbling centuries. It was sad, disillusioned, yet eagerly joyous. It had tasted all things and found them vanity, yet pursued an unending quest with infinite zest.

"Dear Dita," he murmured, "never doubt that I loved you, love you still, but as the artist loves, not the plodder. You or any woman can only be to him the 'shadow of the idol of his thought,' the mere symbol of beauty, but what he really loves, Dita, is beauty's self."

Before she knew it, his arms were about her.

He spoke now with a sincerity almost stern. "You or all the world may think me false," his head lifted lightly, "it is nothing to me. To the one thing I know as truth I am eternally true. I really, fundamentally do not care that," he snapped his fingers, "for the rest of the show. I have always the dream and before me lies the great achievement. So out of your house, out of your life, out of your heart I go." He came near her as he spoke, his voice was like music. Before she knew it, his arms were about her and he was kissing her hair, where the copper shadows rippled into gold above her temple. "Beautiful and still loved Perdita! Good-by."

CHAPTER XXIV

WAITING FOR PERDITA

Perdita committed an unpardonable social sin that evening. She, the hostess, was late in her own house. In fact she had sent down word that they were to begin dinner without her.

The three of them then, Maud, Wallace Martin and Hepworth were sitting gazing at one another in a rather mournful and embarrassed fashion, when Mr. and Miss Fleming were announced. Fuschia had stipulated that she was only to remain with them until the appearance of the roast. That was the signal for her departure, the definite limit of her stay. She was due at the theater before eight and it was her custom never to eat anything before the evening performance. This was the first time any of the group had seen her since her tremendous success of a few evenings before.

"Hands up!" she called from the doorway, her gay, delicious voice pealing through the room, "hands up, I say," making an imaginary pistol of her thumb and forefinger and covering the three. "I don't want either your money or your life, but I do insist upon seeing who has blisters on his hands. I shall accept no other proof of friendship."

Hepworth and Martin promptly held up their hands. "I'm entitled to first honors," said Hepworth, "I've sprained both wrists, can't write my signature and have to have my food cut up for me."

"My hands," said Wallace Martin proudly, "are trained. They no longer show wear and tear. You could drive a dagger against them and it would splinter harmlessly. From long practice in trying to make my own plays go by virtue of my own applause they have acquired the substance and fiber of hickory."

"But dear Miss Fleming," cried Maud, "I deserve more credit than they, for I recklessly sacrificed my most beautiful fan. When the curtain went down for the last time and we climbed off our seats and stopped howling, I held in my hand a limp shred of something and discovered that I had beaten my poor, exquisite, fragile fan to bits."

Fuschia's eyes were full of starry twinkles, her smile was a revelation of joyousness. She drew a long, ecstatic breath, "Boys and girls, it was nice, wasn't it?"

"Nice!" exclaimed Hepworth pushing a chair forward for her, "Nice! Is that the only word you can find to express your pleasure in the fact that the curtain rose thirty times amid continuous cheers, and New York simply took you to her heart and hugged you?"

"Good old New York! She knew her own little Fuschia by the strawberry mark on her left arm, didn't she? I heard Caruso sing for the first time the other afternoon, and when they asked me afterward how I liked it, I said I only knew of one thing more heavenly and that was the sound of a great audience clapping and shouting. There's no music like that."

Dinner was announced, and Maud, with a slightly worried expression, began explaining to Fuschia that Perdita had been detained; but as they moved toward the door, Hepworth noticed that Fleming had not stirred from the remote corner he had sought upon entering the room.

"Jim, what is the matter?" said Hepworth with some concern; "you haven't interrupted Fuschia once since she came in and you know it's always a neck and neck race between you to see which can talk the faster?"

"He's been asleep," said Fuschia, taking her seat at the table. "Poor papa! the gay life, you know!"

Fleming eyed her indignantly across the bank of primroses in the center of the board. "The gay life! I've had no sleep since I struck New York, that's true. I've had to keep going, and take these poor little pick-me-ups of cat-naps whenever I can get them; but why? For a week before this great first night, I had to sit up with Fuschia and hold her hand and tell her what an unparalleled success she was going to have and then that night, after all the excitement and anxiety I suffered as her father, and the exhaustion incident upon being first *claqueur*, why she drove me out into the cold, damp, rainy streets with one of your New York blizzards just setting in, to buy her the first morning papers, and since then I've had to celebrate her triumph. I'll tell you what it is, friends, I'm a raveled sleeve of care and no kind sleep to knit me up."

"Do you know what has really happened?" said Fuschia, in calm explanation. "Dear papa can't help putting in those Dumas and Poe touches, but come to me for the straight truth. It's really the funniest thing about papa. His luck always comes right along with mine. Now what do you think?"

"He's made a million since he came to New York," said Wallace Martin.

"Lost the other fellow's million, you mean," said Hepworth with feeling.

"Wrong. It's the most unexpected thing you ever dreamed of," Fuschia's voice was triumphant, "papa's got a social success. Yes," nodding impressively, "just look at him closely and you'll see that he's lost his natural, unconscious man-look. He now has a drawing-room-pet expression and he's wearing his hair differently, and throwing out his chest. Oh, you needn't laugh, Mr. Hepworth, it's true. 'Hyperion curls, the front of Jove himself.' When we were coming on I determined that I would always be very kind to papa. I'd never neglect nor ignore him, no matter how famous I became; but, of course, he'd just be Fuschia Fleming's father. But what are the real facts of the case? Father sits in the seats of the mighty, flattered by great ladies and avoids mention of his humble actress daughter. King Cophetua and the chorus girl!"

"I had to come to New York to find out that the feminine boycott against me wasn't complete," said Mr. Fleming with emotion. "I tell you, Hep, it's a wonderful experience suddenly to realize that the entire crew of petticoats the world over don't look at you as if they all had glass eyes in their heads instead of real ones."

"How do you account for it, Jim?" asked Hepworth.

"From camp to court, my boy, has ever been but a step, although sometimes it's a mighty long one," returned Fleming oratorically. "Now this is the way I've explained it to myself. You see, I've got that wild, free, above-timber-line flavor about me that simply locos the type of woman that keeps husband hobbled to a stake under the big tree by the back porch where she can keep an eye on him from the kitchen windows. Now, personally, the catnip and parsley kind of woman never did appeal to me; but these New York orchids are different. They know how to appreciate the Rocky Mountain edelweiss, and seem grateful to me for taking their husbands off their hands now and then. And they're so interested, too, in the little every-day incidents of an old prospector's life."

"You just ought to hear papa Othelloize those Ophelias," said Fuschia, deftly seizing the first opportunity to get into the conversation. "He'll tell them about being carried down a thousand feet in a mighty snowslide and escaping unhurt, and of the fabulous properties he's discovered, and of frequent encounters with enormous grizzlies, where he'll tap them lightly on the jaw and advise them to hasten home and then if they get too familiar, he gives them a twist of the wrist that sends them howling back to the woods."

"Fuschia," said her father sternly, "you talk entirely too much, and there's a day of reckoning coming for you. Just wait till you get to London. There you'll be sneaking in at the back door and eating a cold biscuit in the pantry while you're waiting to do a few recitations for the ladies and gentlemen; while I'll be sailing in to dinner with a belted earless on one arm and a tiaraed duchess on the other."

"I'm afraid I see your finish, Jim," sighed Hepworth. "You'll end as a leader of cotillions. Your head is badly turned."

"There's no denying, Hep, that we are apt to set and undue value on what we've never had, and these late-blooming feminine smiles are like a bottle of champagne in the desert."

"Oh, dear, here is the roast," cried Fuschia disconsolately, "and Cinderella must run away. Is there no hope of seeing Mrs. Hepworth this evening?" turning to Maud.

Maud hesitated a moment, then, "I really do not know," she confessed frankly, "she—she has not been particularly well all day." She simply could not plead for Perdita the conventional bad headache while Hepworth's steady eyes were fixed upon her.

Fuschia, who happened to be looking at him, saw a quick shade of disappointment pass over his face, and her impulsive sympathy was roused by the depth and poignancy of that immediately suppressed emotion. She threw herself into the breach.

"Oh, I want dreadfully to see her to-night about the gown I am to wear when I play the scheming adventuress next week. We were to have decided it to-night. She is thinking of putting me in green instead of the usual black with touches of scarlet, and the accustomed badge of the adventuress, high-heeled scarlet slippers. And I am so anxious to know if Mrs. Hepworth has decided upon green, a wonderful, wicked, dazzling green, with strange blue lights in the shadows. Oh, may I send a message and ask her to see me just a moment?"

But before Maud could answer, Perdita entered the room. She pleaded the usual headache, which Maud had so carefully avoided, and that threadbare social fiction was for once upheld and substantiated. Dita's appearance fully bore it out. Her face was pale, her eyes heavy. She promised, however, to give a full consideration to the question of Fuschia's green gown the next morning, and the actress who had already overstayed the limits of the time she had allotted herself prepared to take her departure.

"Oh," she cried from the door, "I forgot to announce my two important bits of good news. Mr. Martin is going to write me a comedy and Eugene Gresham is going to paint my portrait."

A faint smile hovered for one moment about Perdita's lips. "When did Eugene make his request?" she asked in her usual low tones, although her head lifted suddenly.

"This afternoon," replied Fuschia, and Dita's smile deepened. "And he is going to give me a fête in his studio."

"The usual ball in the artist's studio?" laughed Maud looking at Martin.

"Don't you dream it," Fuschia laughed irrepressibly, also; "not the stage kind with its crowd of maskers. This is to be patterned after an afternoon among the great artists in Japan. You wear Japanese things and crawl through a little door into a room with nothing in it but just one perfect flower in a perfect vase, and we will all sit on the floor and drink tea."

"It sounds very much like him," said Maud, "but is it true Wallace that you are really going to do a play for Miss Fleming?"

"It happily is," said Martin, "a comedy."

"Not a problem play?" The light of hope dawned in Miss Carmine's eyes.

"Oh, dear me, no," cried Fuschia; "and he's going to write it just as he talks."

"I'd very much prefer to have you talk it as I write," said Martin, but she had already vanished.

In a very few minutes the others followed her example, Fleming leaving the house with Maud and Wallace.

213

CHAPTER XXV

WITH MY HEART'S LOVE

Scarcely had the hall door closed behind them when Hepworth turned to Dita inquiringly. "Would you not very much prefer that I left you?" he asked. "I can see that you are not well, and we can discuss anything that remains to be talked over at any other time."

"No," she shook her head, "I am quite well. I have not even the headache I claimed, and I must, indeed I must, talk to you tonight."

"But if our conversation this morning so upset and unnerved you," he urged, "would it not be wise to defer this?"

"Our conversation didn't," she replied with emphasis. "It was another conversation. Cresswell, will you answer me a question or two?"

"Anything you wish to know," he replied.

She got up, and, after a fashion she sometimes showed, perhaps unconsciously copied from him, began to walk restlessly up and down, occasionally stopping to pick up and examine some ornament quite as if she had never happened to notice it before.

She had picked up a small jade vase from the mantelpiece and was now bestowing upon it what appeared to be an exhaustive observation. In reality she was hardly conscious that she held it in her hand.

"Cresswell, why did you marry me?"

He started ever so slightly and then answered unhesitatingly, "Because I loved you, Dita."

A little spasm of some emotion he could not fathom passed over her face. "It was not because you wished to see how the flower blooming in a tin can in a tenement window would bloom in a wonderful lacquered vase in a marble court? It was not from curiosity or pity, Cresswell?"

"It was love, Dita."

Again that wave of emotion over her face, and then she looked about her with sad, tear-wet eyes and a trembling mouth.

"And my caprices, my stupidity, my inadequacy, soon destroyed that?"

"Never," he repeated. "Believe that. I was no gardener trying experiments. It was the flower I loved, Dita; the flower whose happiness I longed for, whose happiness I still long for. You do not need my love, do not care for it, why should you? But give me the happiness of still being able to assure for you the marble courts and the lacquered vases."

The little jade vase dropped from her fingers and fell unheeded to the rug at her feet. The tears were pouring now, down her white face. She made no effort either to conceal or to staunch them.

"Ah, blind and wasteful creature that I am!" she cried. "Why, why should you have chosen to love me?"

She stepped toward him and with both hands unwound the slender old-fashioned gold chain from her throat. She lifted her face, quivering, broken with feeling, and still streaming with tears, to his. She held out the amulet toward him. "Cresswell," poignantly, "will you take this now, my old talisman, with my heart's love?"

He made one quick movement as if to take her in his arms and hold her close, close to his heart for ever. His face was irradiated, his cold eyes glowed with a warmth and fire that more mercurial and mutable natures can never know.

Then the light went out of his eyes and face. It did not fade, it was as if it were extinguished by some strong effort of will. His arms fell to his sides.

"My dear, my dear," his voice trembled, "how like your sweet, generous, prodigal nature! I see it all now, the reason for your pallor and heavy eyes. You have spent the day, since I left you this morning, in accusing and denouncing yourself until you have reached the frame of mind where you can only appease your offended and tyrannical conscience by some act of high sacrifice. And do you think I would accept it, poor, heroic, overwrought Dita? All day," that swift, flashing, heart-breaking smile of his gleamed a moment, "you have been convicting yourself of ingratitude, merely because I was offering you some of my money with the entirely selfish motive of securing my own happiness."

"You are wrong, wrong," she cried vehemently, passionately. "What can I do to convince you? Oh, of course, you think that I am a creature of moods; you have every reason to think so; but what can I do, what can I say to convince you that I am not speaking from one of them now?"

"Say nothing, dearest," he murmured deeply, soothingly; "say no more. I shall always remember the sweetness of this moment."

"But I will not have it so," she cried. "You must, you must listen to me. You think that I love Eugene, that I have always loved Eugene. And I did not know, I did not know what love was. Eugene is charming and famous, and there was a sympathy between us, on one side of our natures. We have the same love of color. It is a passion with us. It spells music and poetry and all sorts of untranslatable things. It is something instinctive with us, something we were born with and we see shades and harmonies and values that other people do not. But this absolute understanding between us was only on one side of our natures, and yet sometimes it was so—so encompassing that I thought it embraced them all. So I did not know my own mind. I was puzzled, confused, always in doubt. And then, when I began really to—to flirt with Eugene, or so people construed it, it was when I was beginning to be bored with my marble court and my lacquered vase. I got so bored with being amused, just amused all the time."

"Ah, that was where I made my great, my unforgivable mistake," he interrupted.

"Yes, you made a mistake, in not letting me know you as you really are," she conceded, "but then, with all the boredom, I had that sense of futility, of failure behind me. Failure behind and nothing to look forward to but an endless succession of marble courts. No beautiful, dazzling unexpected. Just the same thing over and over and over. And then you went away and for a time I was frightened and forlorn, so Maud and I started our venture. Ah!" she clasped her hands together, the amulet dangling on its chain, "I have told you what work and success meant to me. You understand that; but gradually, as I got used to it, I began to see that it wasn't enough. No," she shook her head sadly, "it wasn't enough—there must be love. But I had got the idea into my head that it was Eugene who would speak the magic word, that magic word that I believed in and waited for. Yet all, all the time, from the moment you left me, you were in my thoughts. You see," with a faint smile, "I understood Eugene, but you were the unsolvable problem. I was always thinking about you, trying to understand you, and last night," her face glowed with a lovely light, "when you talked to me of the big, wonderful things, when you made me feel that I was an intelligent human being and not merely a pretty woman, why, my whole heart went out to you and I knew it was you, you alone that I loved. It is not the man who can conquer a city, many cities, with his grace and charm and genius. Not he who can win my poor heart, but the man who can conquer his own spirit. Ah, Cresswell," she held out the amulet again to him, "will you not take this now?" "Perdita!" he cried deeply and held her close.

End of the book.